Minister's Guide to FINANCIAL PLANNING

Minister's Guide to FINANCIAL PLANNING

Kenneth M. Meyer

Foreword by D. Stuart Briscoe

Ministry Resources Library

Zondervan Publishing House • Grand Rapids, MI

Minister's Guide to Financial Planning
Copyright © 1987 by Kenneth M. Meyer

Ministry Resources Library is an imprint of Zondervan Publishing House, 1415 Lake Drive, S.E., Grand Rapids, Michigan 49506.

Library of Congress Cataloging-in-Publication Data

Meyer, Kenneth M.
    Minister's guide to financial planning / Kenneth M. Meyer.
        p.   cm.
    Bibliography: p.
    ISBN 0-310-34621-5
    1. Clergy–Finance, Personal. I. Title.
BV4397.M49   1987
332.024'2—dc 19   87-22165
                                              CIP

Statements in this book regarding investments are not to be considered buy, sell, or hold recommendations, but express only the personal opinions of the author.

Edited by James E. Ruark
Designed by Louise Bauer

Printed in the United States of America

87 88 89 90 91 92 / EP / 10 9 8 7 6 5 4 3 2 1

*This book is dedicated to Keith and Kevin,
sons by birth, clergy by call and by choice.*

CONTENTS

FOREWORD

Kenneth Meyer does not waste words; neither does he evade issues. Having been a pastor for many years and more recently having served Trinity Evangelical Divinity School as president, he is well aware of the special pressures of ministry, not least in the matter of finances.

It has been fashionable for ministers not to talk about money except as it relates to everyone but themselves, but this has resulted in many ministers getting themselves into deep trouble. Meyer states, "A call to ministry [does] not include financial security. For most it has proved to be continuing financial jeopardy." This book was written to help stem the tide of pastors leaving the ministry in large numbers because of financial problems.

To those who may feel "pangs of guilt" for even considering their financial security (or presumably purchasing this book), the author offers soothing words of encouragement. For those contemplating a call to ministry there are surprisingly straightforward words of advice on how to negotiate a working arrangement that, if done properly, can save a lot of problems further down the pike. The harassed spouses of starting pastors who are trying hard to manage on less are treated to pithy pieces of advice on garage sales and supermarkets. (I didn't know that if two people shop together they spend more than if shopping separately!)

When I first became a pastor I was amazed that all the people who came to visit me sold insurance. Slowly it dawned on me that they were looking, not for fellowship, but for business. I could have used the helpful details on insurance contained in this book. I'm glad to see that I made the right decision on home ownership many years ago—but not without holding my breath and wondering if I had done the right thing. Pastors reading Meyer's section on home ownership need not hold their breath.

It should be pointed out, however, that giving a book on ministers' finances to a minister without giving a copy to the church board is like preaching to women about submission without ever getting around to telling the men to love their wives. There are two sides to the subject of minister's finances, and this book should also be read by the boards who care for those who are in the ministry.

For too long churches have worked on the principle, "If the Lord keeps the minister humble, we'll keep him poor." Blessed indeed is the minister who is loved by the congregation so much that they support him in such a way that he can do his work without financial stress, and doubly blessed is he if he reads this book and learns how to handle his resources well.

D. Stuart Briscoe
Waukesha, Wisconsin

PREFACE

Clergy face a particular dilemma. They are to be deeply committed to the "spiritual" by reason of call and vocation, but are forced to live in the real world of the material, of dollars and sense.

This dichotomy is complicated by the fact that our mates and children are always affected by this dilemma.

I entered the ministry in a day when laypeople expected clergy to preach, bury, marry, counsel, and administer the sacraments, but certainly not engage in the business and financial matters of the church. A generation later, laypeople are asking whether seminaries teach students anything about finances or running a small business. This 180-degree turn is acknowledgment that in a real sense, every clergyman who serves as a pastor becomes the CEO (chief executive officer) of what amounts to a small business.

The major concern of this volume is not the management of a church and its finances, but the personal management of family finances. These are not completely separate entities in terms of financial stewardship for clergy.

Brian Griffiths's outstanding volume *The Creation of Wealth* (InterVarsity, 1985) expresses the challenge succinctly: "The Christian church has never found it easy to come to terms with the market place." If this is true in a broad sense, it is certainly accurate in the particular—the clergy's personal finances. It just doesn't seem spiritual to be concerned about money and finances.

Only in recent years have clergy begun to reach a level of salary that offers fair compensation for the education and responsibility they bring to their vocation. Even now, such compensation is spotty and inconsistent, with some clergy approaching six figures in salary and benefits while others live on food stamps. This guide is not a call to equalizing salaries—not at all—but it is a clarion to both high- and low-scale clergy to deal biblically and knowledgeably with the resources of their personal finances. It also calls laypeople to greater accountability in dealing with clergy compensation.

We must live by faith, but still exercise planning that works toward financial security. Faith and financial planning cannot be considered incompatible. Financial problems in the parsonage deeply affect the pulpit and ministerial practice.

I have had the privilege as president of Trinity Evangelical Divinity School of conferring theological degrees on nearly three thousand potential clergy. God has also blessed me with two sons in Christian ministry, both serving as pastors. This book is written with the hope that my two sons by blood and my thousands of "sons and daughters" in clergy responsibilities will be better stewards of the resources God allows them so that they in turn will be free to serve without the threat of economic collapse or disaster.

Finally, I offer a personal word. My first parish was a newly planted church—five members—and during those years I was bivocational, a "tentmaker," to use the contemporary phrase. It was not easy to serve a new church, a wife, and a child. The salary was minimal, and to furnish our home we borrowed against our only insurance policy; but we learned lessons in financial accountability and responsibility that have stood us in good stead. I subsequently served congregations as large as two thousand. The salary packages changed in those years, but the principle remained constant with the parable of the talents: we are responsible as God's stewards, God's economists, for all that He gives us—gifts, talents, and dollars.

My hope to clergy readers is that this book may do four things for you and your family. First, make you aware of your fiscal responsibilities as a spiritual aspect of life.

Second, cause you to sit down and review, evaluate, and plan with your mate financially. Third, clean up and clear up financial matters that are not well tended to or could be improved. Fourth, secure a bit more peace and joy for your financial future and ultimately save, through one or more suggestions, the cost of this book tenfold!

ACKNOWLEDGMENTS

Any volume is more than the work and effort of the author. This book is the result of the dedication and work on both typewriter and computer by my administrative assistant, Mrs. Dorothy Branding, and my wife, Carol. My deepest thanks to both of them for making this book possible.

1 | A BIBLICAL CASE FOR FINANCIAL PLANNING

Should the title for this chapter ever be in the form of a question? Certainly not for any serious student of Scripture. Yet we live as clergy in a world where for decades sound financial planning was a breach of our faith commitment: Isn't God going to take care of missionaries and pastors?

There are still clergy today who feel pangs of guilt concerning their interest in financial planning, that guilt carried over from a false dichotomy that separates the spiritual from the material.

Obviously the Bible has much to say about our stewardship of life, including our material resources. Clergy, above all, should know the biblical foundations of Christian stewardship and exhibit a biblical perspective that will affect their professional influence, personal performance, and family well-being.

"Biblical stewardship" has been defined in various ways. Cecil A. Ray states succinctly, "Christian stewardship is the ordering and shaping of the whole life in accordance with the will of God as revealed in Jesus Christ.[1]

My own definition of Christian stewardship is "the recognition that the believer is accountable for all of life's resources as invested by God and that we act as managers and not owners of these resources." That is, the steward (believer) is responsible to the owner (God) for all resources,

---

1. Cecil A. Ray, *How to Specialize in Christian Living* (Nashville: Convention Press, 1982), p. 44.

and especially for those given individually. The Greek word *oikonomos*, from which we derive the terms "economy" and "economist," means "steward" or "household manager" and can be expanded to carry the meaning of "caretaker of another's possessions for profit."

The Old Testament recognized the stewardship of life as far back as the Creation, when Adam was instructed to care for the environment. It was emphasized further through the Mosaic civil laws, which issued regulations on many aspects of the economy—including usury and credit—and provided for the special care of the priests and Levites by the faithful. The Old Testament society recognized the steward-ship of resources under the sovereign guidance of the Jehovah God.

In the New Testament, the parables of Jesus and the Sermon on the Mount are a rich source of material on principles for biblical financial planning. The parable of the talents in Matthew 25:14–30 is one example. Jesus told of a landowner who, as he is about to depart on a journey, calls together three trusted stewards and gives them instructions about managing his property and finances. The point of the story is that two of the three planned to manage the money entrusted to them; the third was condemned because he made no financial plans and did not use the money to advantage. He was harshly rebuked because he simply did not exercise wise handling of the funds for the owner's profit. He was not a good steward.

There are a number of significant economic ideas in this parable. The master "entrusted his property" to the stewards (v. 14). Obviously the parable emphasizes the faith the owner placed in his managers. Note also the immediacy of investment on the part of the first two: "went at once and put his money to work" (vv. 16–17). There was no lingering, no waiting for a more convenient time or place, but a plan put into operation immediately.

An additional thought is that the owner recognized the different abilities and gave different amounts: "each accord-ing to his ability" (v. 15). So even resources are given by God unequally, but with the same measure of accountability. A final observation calls attention to the fact that the one-talent manager made only one choice—to do nothing, dig a hole, and bury the money. The other two made choices and planned. The rebuked servant simply did not act and was called "wicked and lazy." The servant sought to justify himself in saying, "so I was afraid" (v. 25). It is hoped that this book will remove some of the fears and anxieties you may have so that you will be the servants that hear the commending words, "Well done, good and faithful servant" (vv. 21, 23).

The following principles can be found in the parable:

1. God "entrusts" resources to us in many forms, especially financial.
2. God gives these resources to His servants in different quantities ("according to his abilities").
3. God expects us to plan and manage for profit.
4. God condemns "laziness" or "anxiety" in our planning, as He did in the harsh rebuke of the one-talent manager.
5. God holds each manager equally accountable. None is excused even though the distribution is five times greater for one than for another.
6. God's work is advanced or hindered by the way we plan our financial stewardship.

Financial principles are not limited to one parable of Jesus. A survey of Scripture reveals similar expectations of wise financial planning in the parables of the dishonest steward (Luke 16:1–13) and the wise and foolish servants (Luke 12:42–48). As in the parable of the talents, the emphasis is always on accountability.

A believer's accumulation of resources must encounter the warnings of the Sermon on the Mount when Christ (Matt. 6:19–34) admonishes His followers not to be worried about food, clothing, or other material needs. Are clergy who purchase nonessentials or who accumulate money toward retirement under indictment according to Christ's teachings? Obviously, I don't believe so.

The emphasis of Christ in this passage is on the priority

and motivation that any servant of God places on materialism. The emphasis of verse 24—"You cannot serve both
God and Money" (NIV)—is that one must decide to whom
he is responsible and owes worship. If our goal in life is
simply to accumulate things and wealth, we have fallen prey
to the trap of materialism and are duly rebuked by Christ's
words. If our devotion and highest motivation are to serve
God, whatever the cost, then our priorities and motivation
are correct and not under condemnation, even if accumulated resources abound.

The early church certainly had servants who were
within God's will, yet had accumulated resources—for
example, Lydia and Philemon—but they gave their devotion
and priority to serving the Lord.

Clergy must be especially careful to keep material
resources in balance. The end of life is not the accumulation
of wealth, but approval of God. The secular world too often
faults clergy for monetary motivation. As clergy we must
live in respect to Christian stewardship and accountability.

There is no disputing that there is great variance in
pastors' salaries and benefits. That circumstance, however, is
relatively unimportant to the biblical principles stated.
Accountability is a factor to be faced by all.

It is also true that clergy today receive better compensation in terms of salary and benefits than at any other time in
this century. Yet mismanagement can characterize the pastor
in the high-salaried superchurch as well as the pastor in the
rural or inner-city parish who must get by on the most
meager pay. Responsibility for financial planning is not
determined by the amount of salary. More money does not
mean better management.

Before any clergy criticizes the church, berates the
leadership, or bemoans the lack of dollars available at the end
of the month, he must honestly face the question, have I
practiced biblical principles in my financial management and
planning?

As we confront this question, let us examine financial
management and planning as "managers of His possessions
for profit."

2 | *STAGES OF CLERGY'S FINANCIAL LIFE*

Gail Sheehy writes in *Passages* about the sociological stages we pass through in human living. We can readily recognize that there are also "passages" or stages in our financial condition.

I acknowledge five basic financial stages in a minister's adult life. The phases are certainly not definitive, but pragmatic. Nor are they uncommon in other professions.

INSTRUCTION/APPRENTICE STAGE (AGE 18 TO SEMINARY GRADUATION)

The outer limits of the first stage are not clearly defined. This is primarily due to the "late" age at which many ministerial students enter seminary, either for financial reasons or in making career changes. It is barely possible anymore to "put oneself through" college and seminary. Many clergy graduate from seminary with education loans totaling as much as $20,000! The debt service on these loans over ten years is enormous and will require payments exceeding $230 per month. The seminary graduate faces this debt as a fixed cost for the first ten years of ministry; thus a young clergyman faces a large debt payment at a low-paying stage of life. This affects the young pastor and his family and places a burden on the church.

This may seem to be a bleak scenario, but as a seminary administrator I see it unfold time and time again. The cost of undergraduate and graduate education is staggering. The outlook for improvement is not encouraging.

How can the problem of indebtedness be overcome? A solution may lie in a combination of factors.

1. The student/student family may choose to extend a normal three-year program to four or five years, combining additional work income with fewer hours spent in the classroom. Many theological institutions have watched the "normal" three-year master's program become the exception, and the four-plus years of education the norm. Institutions with a quarter system provide a more flexible program for the financially burdened student, since quarters allow short or frequent hiatuses more easily than a semester system. "Block courses" (all classes limited to two or three days a week) may offer better scheduling for part-time jobs.

2. A concerted plan by the "sending church" and theological institution to provide financial aid is needed. A growing number of churches is recognizing this responsibility and providing partial scholarships. Church financial support of students from the congregation may be the only way some "called" to ministry will be able to complete their education.

Some churches will consider financial support only after graduation, especially if the person is committed to overseas missions. I believe training is worthy of investment, too, but there can be complications. The last fifteen years have produced a high percentage of theological students who came to faith or were called to the ministry late in their college years or through a parachurch ministry. These students may not have established a denominational connection or a church home, and therefore they come to seminary without the encouragement and support of that kind of community.

The cost of education also reaches beyond this first stage. The cost of books, which are the tools of the trade, as well as the level of dress and entertainment expected of clergy may come as a shock during the transition from apprentice to full vocational ministry. Many seminary students have come to their senior year with one business suit or perhaps a sport coat or two. It is a vocational and financial reality that a clothing budget for most clergy will require more than one business suit! These factors affect the financial aspect of the first church, the first call. Entry-level salaries have certainly improved, but would probably range on average in 1987 between $15,000 and $24,000, based on geography, economic environment, and the size of the church. These kinds of salaries dictate that careful attention be given to budgeting and economizing.

I suggest that it is a wise student who considers buying a basic life insurance program while still in seminary. A term life insurance policy for $100,000 today, if the student is under age thirty, should not cost more than about $120 per year. Any policy for less than $100,000 is, in my opinion, less than full value for cost.

Now we are ready for the next stage, and here both the opportunities and problems are compounded.

FORMULATION STAGE
(GRADUATION TO AGE 40)

Not only are theology and philosophy of ministry in a formative state during the second phase, but so is our financial plan and program. Fiscal habits made during this formulative period are not easily broken. The spendthrift at thirty will not suddenly change character and habit at fifty.

Financially this period sees not only growth, but adjustment. The salaries of most clergy will have doubled or more by forty years of age compared with their salaries in the first three years of ministry.

The other side of the issue is that the same person will have financial needs that grow at or faster than the pace of the salary.

This is the time for all clergy to set financial goals, live within a budget, and begin planting financial seeds for the future. This is also the stage when growth may come rapidly in income, but also in expenses. This phase will be marked by a number of consumer expenses—care of children, medical care, clothing, automobile—all of which will cost more than the Internal Revenue Service (IRS) ever thought of allowing for deductions. Furniture that will hopefully remain for years will be a major investment. Savings must be foundational to any plan.

My experiences in financial planning seminars have revealed that stress over finances is greater during this stage than at any other time for clergy. I have observed that not a few clergy have come to their fortieth birthdays without three months' salary in ready savings available. A "hand-to-mouth" existence seems normal and puts enormous stress on the marriage and also on the ministry. I believe that the majority of clergy who "drop out" before age forty do so for financial reasons, or the financial problems have been at least a contributing factor.

Investments are most important for future financial stability. A hundred dollars a month invested from age twenty-five and compounded at 10 percent interest produces a staggering amount by age seventy. Money compounded at 10 percent doubles every seven years. This initial $1,200 for the first year thus reaps in excess of six doublings. The result in dollars is that the first year's $1,200 has now compounded to more than $40,000 at seventy years of age. Yet few clergy feel they can commit themselves to such a beginning. Yet they must seek to do so for a satisfactory retirement.

Remember, our financial future is not easily built after forty-five. It is greatly determined by the investments made in the years before.

This crucial stage of formulation in reality sets the direction for our tomorrows. Setting financial priorities is essential. Denial today may result in deferred enjoyment and peace of mind.

THE ACCUMULATION/INVESTMENT STAGE (AGES 40 TO 55)

Things accumulate, not only in the personal attic, but also in the financial area during the third stage of life. Debt accumulates, often too rapidly and easily, in the form of house payments, car loans, education for children, and for some, short-term loans for consumer needs. The accumulation stage is the time when the "credit card syndrome" strikes hard. Although there is a need to establish credit with one or two credit cards, it can be a fatal trap. Treat the credit card as one month's cash, and never allow the credit card to purchase short-term needs or wants on an extended payment. I was horrified to see a pastor in his forties pay for seventy dollars' worth of groceries with a Visa card. I doubt that his entire Visa account was settled without interest charges of 15 to 21 percent. To gauge the effect of this, add 15 to 20 percent to his food bill—the thought is staggering!

This stage should also have positive accumulations, such as home equity (beware of home equity loans for consumer purchases), insurance protection, retirement funds, and possibly additional income sources. Net worth should start to grow, and freedom from financial worries should mark the latter part of this stage. At its end the relief from college expenses is finally in sight, the last wedding bill has probably been paid, grandchildren are coming along, and house payments are now taking a smaller percentage of total income.

The spouse may well consider resuming or expanding a career outside that of homemaker. Long-dreamed-of vacations are not only envisioned, but become reality.

Yet there may be a dark side to these years. The visions of success at thirty-five may need to be adjusted and tuned to the reality of one's ministry. Depression easily sets in. Financial concerns may only add to this problem.

The last and major pastoral move may come at the latter years of this stage. "Early marriage" furniture that bears the scars of children's play is often replaced by a visit to a more exclusive store.

A negative factor in this definitive stage is that clergy friendships initiated in the crucible years of the thirties may loosen or become strained over size of church, position within the denomination, and general economic differences.

One pastor's wife told me she could no longer bear to visit certain seminary friends. The friends had served a large church for some seven years, while this couple's own church size and economic condition had not greatly improved over the last decade. The wife simply felt that the material differences evident when visiting their friends were too hurtful to handle. Perhaps both couples needed to learn something about the grace and true value of possessions.

ACCUMULATION/CONSERVATION STAGE (AGE 55 TO RETIREMENT)

"Conservation" is the code word for the fourth stage. How do we best conserve what has been accumulated? Clergy at this age change financial goals and establish a new concept of financial planning. Although growth is expected in the investment portfolio, now the goal becomes retention and limited growth with minimum risk. Safety with some growth is a better strategy than growth with volatility.

Retirement looms, and a number of decisions must be reviewed. How will we plan for an active and meaningful retirement? Where will we live? Is our health/medical coverage adequate? Should we diminish life insurance coverage in light of the accumulation of retirement funds? What will be my real dollars, after inflationary increases, when I retire? I consider it wise to plan for an attrition, due to inflation, of about 50 percent in real dollars for every ten years after retirement. If the attrition is less, what a happy surprise!

Let me offer an illustration. Suppose I will retire in ten years with accumulated resources of $250,000 in real dollars. That nest egg would be equal to $125,000 today based on an inflation factor of 5 percent per year. The question is, would I be willing to live on the interest produced by $125,000, plus social security, if I were retiring today? The real dollars on today's market for me, including investment income and social security, would be between $21,000 and $25,000 per year! The large amount today may well be eroded, due to inflation, so why not plan for it in this retention period?

Would it not be wise to cut back on our standard of living enough in the last ten years prior to retirement so that "retirement income shock" will not be drastic?

This stage is marked by financial freedom and a much narrower financial focus. At its end we should be financially ready for retirement, not only because of what we have done at this stage, but in the years past.

ENJOYMENT/EXPECTATION STAGE (RETIREMENT)

Americans are living longer, and clergy seem to lead the way on those actuary tables. Most wives will outlive their husbands by a number of years. The pastor who is fifty years old now will probably live until his middle eighties, and his spouse to nearly ninety.

Longevity has a disadvantage, of course, in that our retirement investment may have to carry us longer. Retirement at sixty-five means living off retirement income for as long as twenty years. That is as much as ten years longer than retirement expectancy just a generation or two ago. We cannot count on social security alone to carry us through. And the longevity means additional inflationary chunks out of our income. Yet housing, food, and clothing costs might stay even or decline in these later years.

We must plan for retirement wisely. Chapter 13 deals with the details of this.

Understanding these five stages of financial living makes planning for the future more purposeful and practical. That is the place to begin.

3 | NEGOTIATING THE CALL

Negotiating the call of a clergyman? How can one even speak in those terms in relationship to God's work? Isn't the "called one," the clergy, to accept whatever is offered and be thankful?

After thirty years in the ministry, I answer simply no. There is no reason why God's work must be slipshod and without agreement in some form. Most churches do business with others by written agreement or contract, yet contracts or written agreements with ministerial staff are often regarded as "unspiritual."

A LETTER OF AGREEMENT

I prefer to talk in terms of a "letter of agreement" signed each year by the clergy and the proper board or officers. Such a letter protects both the clergy and the church from misunderstandings that can produce serious conflicts. Renewing the letter of agreement annually also entails two important consequences: (1) an annual review of the financial aspects of the call, and (2) an annual evaluation of the clergy's performance. None of God's servants should fear a fair evaluation, but neither should there be one without a salary review. The letter of agreement demands both and is beneficial for both church and pastor.

In some denominations, there are provisions for determining the terms of a call and forms that must be completed and ratified in order for the call to become official. Such procedures make negotiating a call a smoother process.

Let us suppose that Pastor Johnson has candidated for a vacant pastoral position at Deerfield Community Church. If he is a new seminary graduate seeking his first charge, he obviously has little bargaining power to negotiate a call. This is true in any profession. My advice to this person is simply to decide what is the minimal amount that allows him to accept the call, then trust that God will provide for his needs in the ministry. It is harmful if a graduate's expectations are too high. An active seminary or denominational placement service can be very helpful at this point. Graduates should know well in advance the average placement salary and adjust their living expenses accordingly.

Negotiating a call is usually practical after the first pastorate. Church boards must recognize that a call has two aspects to it: (1) the vote of the congregation, and if that is affirmative, (2) the vote of the pastor and his family. A "call" goes both ways!

Why a "letter of agreement"? Such a document, updated annually, removes the likelihood of squabbles, hurts, and misunderstandings. It is good business and administration. Verbal agreements produce misunderstandings and misinterpretations and can be used by Satan to foment division in a congregation.

Leadership changes. If you came to your present pastorate five years ago, consider how many of the original call committee are now a part of the board determining compensation. Probably just a few remain. For consistency, therefore, a written agreement is helpful.

Some laypeople may regard this concept as less than spiritual and too businesslike. Yet they would seek a comparable agreement if they were seeking an administrative position in nonreligious work.

Finally, the letter of agreement should mandate an annual review of the pastor's ministry. This evaluation is necessary for all clergy. It should be a time of supportive encouragement and helpful criticism. Never should it be viewed as confrontational, but as confirming and consultative. Too often a pastoral evaluation is made only when there is dissatisfaction with his ministry; by mandating an annual review, the letter of agreement averts a crisis atmosphere.

The agreement should be prepared in triplicate and signed by both the pastor and the proper board or congregational authorities. One copy is retained by the clergy and one by the present chairman or moderator, and the third is included in the official minutes of the church.

TERMS OF THE CALL

Certain items should always be included in a letter of agreement.

Cash salary

The cash salary is the amount of compensation less any benefits and allowances—in other words, available cash for daily living expenses.

Housing/housing allowance

If the church provides housing in the form of a parsonage or manse, it is always difficult to evaluate its true monetary value. This depends on the relative cost of housing in the geographic area. Church boards must realize that the financial and tax benefits in a parsonage will never be as great for the clergyperson as home ownership. Boards must also recognize that equity will not be attributed to the minister. Of course, there are offsetting factors such as the fact that the church, not the minister, is liable for repairs, taxes, and the like. More and more churches are giving pastors the option of home ownership.

The advantages and disadvantages of home ownership are examined in chapter 8. A new seminary graduate would be best advised to accept with gratitude a parsonage. There are numerous factors that complicate first-time home ownership. Moreover, the first pastorate requires enough adjustments without the additional problem of buying a home.

Automobile expense

The general business world knows that an automobile is necessary when a job requires being outside the office. Some churches include an amount in their budget that, if not fully amortizing the cost of operation, at least covers the cost of gas and oil and routine maintenance.

Some churches will lease an automobile for the pastor. The financial health of the church and the business acumen of the board will create the climate for automobile purchase or lease. Part of the cost of leasing a car, even when paid by the church, must be reported as income by the pastor. A leased car, under the new tax law, may offer an advantage to the pastor who pays his own auto expenses.

Most churches, especially smaller congregations, still do not consider this expense. It is a wise minister who asks the church to deduct a vehicle allowance from the salary, thus reducing the adjusted gross income and consequently the tax liability. Of course, good record keeping is necessary. Pastors do well to keep track of all mileage and expenses for business purposes. How do we separate personal use from business? Some guidelines are provided in chapter 5.

Books and supplies

Many churches now provide a book allowance placed at the disposal of the pastor. In my last two pastorates, this fund was over and above my salary, amounting in one church to $1,200 per year and in the other, $2,000!

It must be determined in the letter of agreement what kinds of purchases of books and supplies are permissible and who owns these items when the pastoral relationship ends. Most churches will allow these books and/or certain supplies to remain in the possession of the pastor.

Be careful not to obtain books or supplies without proper authorization or under terms not consistent with the letter of agreement. If an allowance is not provided, they may be treated in the same way as automobile expense and deleted from the cash salary, again lowering the taxable income; or they may be treated as a legitimate business expense for self-employed and so listed on the itemized section of the IRS business expense form or Schedule A.

Books have a limited life, and therefore it is important—and legal—to place them on a depreciation schedule of seven to ten years. This treats books like office furniture, even though the value of books in a theological library is difficult to determine in the business of the church. My set of "Keil and Delitzsch" will be as useful for Old Testament studies tomorrow as it was when it was purchased more than twenty years ago. The contents of other books are quite dated, and those volumes have little value after a few years. Therefore the seven-to-ten-year average on depreciation is a fair reckoning.

Entertainment

Entertainment is another category that is difficult to define in regard to taxation. How many times do you entertain? Is it personal or church business? The simple rule to follow is, if I were not the pastor, would I have entertained? Entertaining church guests, new members, missionaries, and denominational leaders, or hosting committee meetings, can be considered legitimate business expense. Under the new tax law, it would be wise to seek monthly reimbursement rather than treating this as a business expense.

Document all business entertainment and its purpose. Record keeping is essential. I suggest having all guests at the parsonage sign a guest book, indicating the date and the purpose. More dollars "slip through" the parsonage budget than we ever realize in the form of business entertainment.

Continuing education

It is shortsighted for a church not to insist on continuing education for its pastoral staff. Other professions emphasize this, so why not the clergy? A number of denominations set standards and requirements for continuing education.

This item should be included in every letter of agreement. The time and expense involved are not personal or "vacation," but a real educational investment that becomes profitable for pastor and church. Some clergy jump from seminar to seminar and call it continuing education. A definite program of continuing education should be considered and then approved by the appropriate church board.

As a seminary president I encourage clergy to investigate the availability of short-term courses on campus or courses by audio tape, video tape, or correspondence. Some clergy will want to plan a program that could lead to a professional degree such as doctor of ministry.

Continuing education should be included in the terms of a call, but whether the cost is borne by the pastor or the church or shared by them may be negotiable.

Vacation

The amount of vacation time should be clearly stated in the letter of agreement and, if there are any calendar restrictions (pertaining to the Christmas or Easter seasons, for example), these should be defined also.

Vacation time will be determined largely by the length of service in ministry. A pastor who has twenty years of experience and has been granted one month's vacation should hardly be expected to accept less time in his next call. Therefore churches must evaluate the "package" the candidate presently receives instead of basing a decision on the former pastor's terms of call.

The following formula might be considered fair to both clergy and church:

> 1–5 years in ministry: two weeks
> 5–10 years in ministry: three weeks
> 10 or more years in ministry: one month

Most denominations will offer suggestions or guidelines for vacation time. This may differ by geographic area or economic situations. Clergy in nondenominational churches might use the guidelines of the denomination that is most compatible with the church theologically.

The pulpit supply during vacation periods should always be reimbursed by the church.

Vacation time often causes conflict. "Workaholics"

often become church leaders and are frustrated that anyone would want to "enjoy" a vacation. In some rural areas farm families are never free from their work. A rural church must recognize professional standards; a suburban "workaholic" must remember that God commanded "rest" as well as "work." Clergy should be aware of and sympathetic to the fact that their vacation time often exceeds the vacation time of church members, even among those who have been in careers longer than they.

Another guideline is that a pastor should not take a vacation week at the church Bible camp or conference. This is not the kind of vacation most clergy need. The Bible camp or conference has a place in the schedule, but not as vacation time. A vacation need not be expensive, but it must be a break from the usual activities of the pastorate.

Some churches are wisely considering granting a study sabbatical after about seven years of service, imitating the common practice of the academic community. Trinity Evangelical Divinity School has a program designed for a clergy sabbatical that consists essentially of a twelve-week exchange between pastor and faculty. The pastor receives a study leave, and the faculty person becomes reacquainted with day-to-day ministry by exchanging certain duties. Other seminaries have comparable plans for alumni.

Full-year sabbaticals may be less profitable than shorter terms. A year is generally too long a time away from the field of action. One pastor-friend found, after a year's sabbatical, that the church was able to function very well without him. He returned only to pack up and move on with an empty feeling for all his successful ministry.

Health and life insurance and annuities

Clergy will be eligible for any denominational pension or annuity plan. In most cases a formula has been established to which each church is asked to conform. Any conditions that do not meet those standards should be noted in the letter of agreement with a statement of goals for improvement.

Some annuities or pensions will be based on the church and the pastor contributing a like amount—perhaps an amount equivalent to 10 percent of the pastor's salary. Ten percent is becoming, in fact, a common standard. Many churches have set a 10-percent contribution as a fair share.

Some aspects of this item will not be mentioned in the letter of agreement. For example, some denominational plans are not "vested" until retirement or age fifty-nine. In other words, the clergy cannot control the funds until retirement; this has distinct disadvantages that will be discussed elsewhere. Clergy in a denominational annuity plan may still opt for a 403(B) (see ch. 10). You should be aware of vestedness and the options open to you even when those matters are not explained in the letter of agreement.

Health insurance is now required by some states in any employer-employee relationship. Most churches consider this an obligation and will pay either the entire amount or a major share. The letter of agreement should specify the financial arrangements.

Some progressive churches are also providing disability insurance. All church boards should include this in the terms of the call. The disability policy protects both the church and the clergy and is well worth the cost. The dilemma and guilt faced by a church when a pastor is disabled are devastating; so are the circumstances of the pastor's family.

Progressive churches are also considering a basic term life insurance policy, paid by the church and kept in force as long as the pastoral relationship continues. A professional liability insurance policy covering both the pastoral staff and the church corporation should be considered.

CONCLUSION

Not every church will be able to include all these benefits in the letter of agreement, but larger churches in particular should treat the pastor in the same businesslike manner as a company's executives and management.

The Bible admonishes, "Let everything be done decently and in order." Somehow this must apply to more than the order of worship.

4 | *THE NEW TAX LAW AND CLERGY*

The income tax has been a permanent part of the United States tax code ever since the Sixteenth Amendment to the Constitution was ratified in 1913—three-quarters of a century ago. The federal tax policy has become over the years far more than a revenue collection to operate government. It is also a tool for implementing social and industrial policy. Deductions of charitable gifts, deductions for home mortgages, escalated appreciation for industrial machinery, oil depletion allowances—all these matters and more have influenced our society in significant ways.

The Tax Reform Act of 1986, which was signed by President Ronald Reagan in October 1986, instituted some of the broadest changes in the income tax since its inception. The changes wrought by this bill will have lasting consequences in our society.

Past reforms of tax policy had a "Band-Aid" effect and closed some loopholes. The Tax Reform Act of 1986 fundamentally reverses the entire direction of tax policy. The law runs to 925 pages.

The new law is complex in many respects, but it probably makes life simpler for lower-income people, since deductions will virtually be eliminated for them and their families.

The complexities will certainly affect stocks and bonds. Some corporations will be hurt by the Tax Reform Act of 1986, but others who were toward the top of the scale in taxes will be paying lower taxes. The prospects at this time are that high-dividend stocks—the "blue chips"—will profit greatly as corporate earnings are turned toward the bottom line and dividends; the blue chips are already rising. This will have impact on clergy pension and retirement plans. It would be prudent to reassess your retirement options and direct funds to mutual funds or stocks that have a goal of equity and income. For the next few years dividends will be as important for performance as for appreciation.

This is a good time to reexamine retirement investments. Most clergy will be vested in a denominational or institutional account, but for those investing independently, this is an important time to make decisions. There is more on this subject in chapter 10.

A second impact of the Tax Reform Act of 1986 lies in charitable giving. The law disallows some deductions but enlarges the tax base, so millions of taxpayers will no longer receive a benefit from charitable gifts unless they itemize deductions.

This situation will have serious consequences for many charitable institutions and nonprofit organizations. It may have less effect on local churches, since giving is more direct and committed. Mission groups, parachurch ministries, seminaries, and Bible colleges may also suffer minimal hurt. Charities that are distant from the "spiritual action" will suffer the most. But all nonprofit organizations will be in a "limbo" period as the tax law takes full effect over the next three to five years.

Not all is doom for the church and charities in the new tax law, however. Now Christians must find their motivation not in tax benefits but in a belief in Christian stewardship. If the Tax Reform Act of 1986 causes more people to give "from the heart" and not for the sake of tax relief, then the church has gained spiritually.

The new legislation is really based on the long-standing desire of a growing number of tax advisers and legislators for a "flat tax"—no loopholes, just a percentage of gross income, hopefully between 10 and 20 percent for the majority. Think of a "flat tax" as synonymous with a sales tax: no matter what product you buy in the local department store, it is taxed at the same rate as anything else. I believe the Tax Reform Act of 1986 will eventually be replaced by a "flat tax" law. While deductions for charity and mortgage interest remain with some changes in the new law, I believe these will eventually be dropped entirely in future legislation. This will greatly affect charitable giving.

The new law restored a benefit for clergy and military personnel. IRS Ruling 83-3 had reduced the housing allowance advantage on homes purchased or built by clergy after January 1983, and the entire benefit was due to be dropped by 1988. But 83-3 has been rescinded. The "double dip" (so-called because tax liability is reduced two ways in the housing allowance) has been fully restored, and ordained or licensed clergy who purchased or bought a home may file an amended tax return for the years 1983 to 1985.

INCOME TAXES

The tax reform promises to lower individual taxes by about $120 billion over the first five years. Individual tax rates are being greatly reduced on a gradual schedule. In 1987 the top rate drops from 50 percent to 38.5 percent, and the number of tax brackets from fifteen to five. In 1988, the highest bracket drops to 28 percent, and the number of brackets drops to just two. This circumstance is expected to keep the "flat tax" concept alive for some time to come.

The new tax structure levies a rate of 15 percent on adjusted gross incomes for married persons with an income up to $29,750, heads of household up to $23,900, and singles up to $17,850.

A tax rate of 28 percent will apply to adjusted gross incomes of $29,750 to $71,900 for married couples filing jointly; $23,901 to $61,650 for heads of household; and $17,851 to $43,150 among singles. An additional 5 percent is added for incomes from $71,900 to $149,250 for married, joint filers; $61,650 to $123,790 for heads of household; and $43,150 to $89,500 for singles. Beyond these amounts the 28 percent tax applies.

By 1989, a family of four with personal exemptions of $2,000 each and a $5,000 zero bracket tax would need to have an adjusted gross income exceeding $13,000 before they would pay any tax. Consider this example for clergy:

$25,000   Salary including housing
 12,000   Housing allowance

$13,000   Adjusted gross income—and no tax!

Let us look briefly at the complicated tax structure for the first few years as the new law is phased in.

1986   Income tax rates (married couples filing jointly)
                  11%—$3,670 ascending to
                  50% for those above $175,250

1987 Tax Rates

Rate	Married	Single
15%	$3,670–28,000	$2,540–16,800
28%	28,000–45,000	16,800–27,000
35%	45,000–90,000	27,000–54,000
38.5%	90,000+	54,000+

1988 Tax Rates

Rate	Married	Single
15%	$5,000–29,750	$3,000–17,850
28%	29,750–71,900	17,850–43,150
33%	71,900–149,250	43,150–89,560
28%	149,250+	89,560+

The new tax law will probably mean many more people will be paying at the 28 percent level. For many clergy there will be increased tax liability—and higher taxes to pay.

Zero Brackets

A zero bracket is a category of adjusted gross income whereby a citizen would pay no taxes. The zero bracket in 1986 is $3,670 for married couples and $2,480 for a single person; in 1987, $3,670 for married persons and $2,540 for singles; in 1988, $5,000 for married and $3,000 for singles. The zero bracket is combined with the new personal exemption schedule.

1986–$1,080
1987–$1,900
1988–$1,950
1989–$2,000

Adjustments on the basis of the consumer price index are promised after 1989. Again, this will allow clergy with a $25,000 salary and a $12,000 housing allowance, reduced from the gross $25,000, to end up with zero tax liability. It is therefore wise for clergy to build into the salary all allowable expenses that lower the salary base.

CAPITAL GAINS

Many clergy will not have to account for capital gains, but for those holding stocks or investments, the new tax law has financial consequences.

The present capital gains law treats asset growth in two categories—short- and long-term gains. Short-term gains offer no tax benefit, but the long-term gains (assets held more than six months) has had 60 percent of its gain excluded. The tax is levied on the remaining 40 percent.

In 1987 the maximum rate for capital assets becomes 28 percent. By 1988, the net capital gain will be added into ordinary income and taxed at the rate of the adjusted gross income. This means that some taxpayers will pay as much as 33 percent on capital gains. This is offset by the right to take up to $3,000 in asset loss against ordinary income. But who anticipates loss of assets?

What does all this mean? First, the change truly simplifies capital gains and losses. Second, it devastates certain tax shelters. Third, there is the advantage of a fine charitable deduction for the value of an asset transferred to a charitable organization. Only time will tell whether these changes in capital gains taxation will have a harmful effect on the stock market and the economy.

INTEREST ON LOANS

The deduction for interest on consumer loans and for finance charges on credit cards and charge accounts is being phased out on the following timetable:

1987	65% of loan interest is deductible
1988	40% is deductible
1989	20%
1990	10%
1991	No loan interest is deductible

Equity loan interest on principal or vacation homes will be deductible if such loans are used for medical or educational costs (such as obtaining a D.Min. degree or putting children through college) within a reasonable time. The loan cannot be used to purchase a new car or other consumer items. The amount of the loan may not exceed the fair market value of the home.

Student loans (as distinct from a home equity loan used for education) are treated as consumer loans, so there is no deduction for interest.

MORTGAGE INTEREST
AND HOUSING ALLOWANCES

IRS Ruling 83-3 states that a minister cannot deduct mortgage interest and property taxes applied to a tax-free parsonage allowance. The new law allows clergy specifically to receive a housing allowance *and* deduct mortgage interest and property taxes. This decision alone probably saves the average clergy home owner from $4,000–$7,000 in taxable income. Clergy with high mortgage payments and in high property tax areas probably will have double the amount saved in taxable income as before.

The guidelines for taking a deduction on the housing allowance must be followed carefully.

- Clergy owning a home must request that the church designate a part of the salary as housing allowance. This must be recorded in the official church minutes.
- The allowance must not exceed the fair market value of home ownership in the community, or its rental value.
- The allowance is not reported on a W2 or 1099 form.
- The allowance must be added to income in determining the social security base.
- The allowance may include principal, taxes, interest, utilities, insurance, maintenance, repairs, and some furnishings.
- The pastor may also claim the interest and property tax on the IRS Schedule A (for itemized deductions).
- Money unspent must be returned to the income line on form 1040. If more money is spent than has been designated, we may not claim the additional expense as an allowance. So it is wise to estimate the high end of the allowance, and if it is not fully spent, it must be put back as income.
- An amended return may be filed for each year from 1983 to 1986 for clergy who purchased or built a home in the period when the double dip was not allowed, but such amendment had to be filed by April 1987.

AUTO EXPENSE

Form 2106 for professional expenses was eliminated in 1987. Car expenses and other professional expenses will now be reported on Schedule A.

The deduction for business use of a car can be calculated at 21 cents a mile up to 15,000 miles, and 11 cents per mile beyond that. When a car reaches 60,000 miles in business use, the depreciation ends.

INVESTMENT INSTRUMENTS

Some investment instruments are affected by tax reform.

403(B) Deferred Tax

Many clergy have wisely opened 403(B) accounts through the church in addition to their denominational retirement accounts. It has advantages for tax deferral (see ch. 10) and is especially useful for employees in educational and charitable (nonprofit) institutions. The new tax law limits the individual's contribution to $9,500; this is more lenient than the 401K plan, which had a limit of $7,000 and is available to profit-making companies and their employees.

Investment Tax Credit

Some clergy have used the deduction for investment tax credit in reference to purchasing a computer or even an automobile that is used exclusively for business. This tax credit has been repealed.

Investment Retirement Accounts

The law on Investment Retirement Accounts (IRAs) is complex. The new law allows an IRA if the employer does not maintain a pension plan. If we have an adjusted gross income that qualifies (under $40,000 for married couples, under $25,000 for singles), we may take the full IRA deduction. The deduction is phased out on the next $10,000 of earnings above the $40,000 (for married) and $25,000 (for single).

I advise clergy to ask their accountants about qualifying for an IRA deduction. It may be a matter of interpretation. If the church does not have a retirement plan and the gross income is low enough, the deduction is probably allowable.

OTHER EFFECTS OF THE LAW

Most of the following provisions of the tax reform took effect in January 1987:

- The deduction for two wage earners for a married couple filing jointly has been repealed.
- All unemployment compensation will be taxed.
- Awards and prizes will be taxable unless assigned to a charitable organization.

- The state and local sales tax deductions are eliminated. This is a major loss of a deduction that amounted to several hundred dollars for most families and was even higher when a car or major appliance was purchased.
- Medical deductions will be allowed only to the extent that the total expenses exceed 5 percent of the adjusted gross income. Modifications to a home for disabled or "handicapped" people will qualify as a medical expense.
- Only 80 percent of the meal cost will be deductible, and bona fide business discussion must take place. Any expenses reimbursed by the church are not deductible.
- Unreimbursed business expenses, professional dues, tax return costs, and some other items will be deductible only if the total amount exceeds 2 percent of the adjusted gross income. Clergy may prefer to have such expenses reimbursed by the church, even if the salary is reduced proportionately. It is better for the church to pay expenses than to have the pastor claim a business expense.
- The $1,500 deduction for adopting children has been repealed.
- The deduction for moving expenses remains for taxpayers who itemize. This is a deduction many clergy overlook, thinking the only eligible cost in moving is the transport of furniture. But other items are allowable, including the cost of motel and meals in travel to the new parish.

CONCLUSION

The Tax Reform Act of 1986 has a direct effect on clergy financial planning. The positive side is the restoration of mortgage interest and taxes as deductible, including the housing allowance. The negative aspects are seen in the fewer and smaller deductions allowable overall. The effect on charitable giving may be severe for some churches and institutions; this may cause churches to be more cautious in offering salary increases. I believe that the new tax law brings us closer to the introduction of a flat tax that will allow no deductions. I believe that will mean simpler tax preparation, but higher taxes for most.

5 | *BUDGETING AND RECORD KEEPING*

Budget making and record keeping go together like the proverbial "love and marriage." These two are the main components of financial stability for whatever one's income may be over the years. Most clergy, like other people, fail in their financial planning at the point of budget and records. The two are inseparably linked.

What is a budget? It is defined in many ways, but the simplest definition may well be the best: A budget is a plan to spend.

Record keeping is hard work, but it is vital because future budgeting is always based on the records of the past year.

GUIDELINES FOR KEEPING RECORDS

There are some guidelines to follow in regard to budget and records.

1. *Designate one member of the family as record keeper and check writer.* Often it is thought that the financial keeper of the books should be the male or husband. But often the wife or woman of the house is better suited for the task. My wife has been the record keeper and check writer for nearly all our married life. Of course, I am aware of the budget and have full checkbook access, but she keeps the books. It is a matter of which person is better with details and which one can

better make the time for the job, which probably amounts to six to ten hours per month. My wife and I jointly make decisions on investments, however. This situation builds mutual trust. We build on the gifts and talents of each other.

2. *Compile a history of the past year's spending.* No matter what the date, start 365 days earlier. Simply enumerate the major categories and, using the checkbook and receipts, list the total expenditures in each category and then the total of all categories for the year. A simple ledger journal will be necessary for this detail.

Analyze the totals in each category. The first purpose is to see where expenses can be cut.

This recap of spending is not a budget, but a history of spending. It will be most enlightening and suggestive of change. Some items will be unchangeable, but others warrant a tough review. For example, many couples will find that expenditures for "entertainment"—which for clergy may simply mean dining out—often take more dollars than anticipated. The overspending may be in some other category. The history will reveal spending areas and is prerequisite to constructing a budget. It will be a painful but therapeutic exercise.

3. *Calculate the total income anticipated for the coming year.* In many cases this will involve only one figure, the clergy's income. But the number of two-income families (the second either full-time or part-time) is increasing in the United States, clergy included. Sometimes the second income will be an estimate; remember not to estimate too high.

Income from fees or honoraria should be categorized as "unanticipated income." Some clergy view such fees as a part of services already covered in the salary, but parishioners should expect to offer a financial gift to the clergy for services such as weddings and funerals. Most churches allow the clergy to keep these fees as personal gifts. A small parish will produce few dollars, and this is income that cannot be anticipated with certainty.

Many clergy will designate these unanticipated funds for a specific purpose such as vacation, spouse's clothing, or entertainment. The main thing to remember is that such income should not be placed on the income side of the ledger; it is an unanticipated bonus.

It is hoped we will not include income from investments, since it should be reinvested and not used to meet budgeted expenses unless we are in retirement.

The total income line must be matched with our annual spending recap. The difference will reveal a negative or positive cash flow. A negative cash flow means some hard evaluation is required in the next step, budget making. A positive cash flow demands investment decisions.

Most clergy will find comparing the spending history with the anticipated income a difficult but revealing exercise. It is necessary for sound financial planning.

4. *Distinguish between fixed and variable expenses.* Fixed expenses include the tithe and offerings, housing costs, utilities, insurance premiums, taxes, and the like. Variable expenses are generally construed to be clothing, household furnishings, entertainment, gifts, and nonprofessional books and magazines.

5. *Record all your expenses on a budget worksheet or ledger journal.* This should include both variable and fixed expenses. Quarterly, semiannual, and annual expenses must be planned in monthly allotments, with the funds to be set aside from each paycheck so that payments can be made on schedule without ballooning the budget expenses.

6. *Keep the records and such items as canceled checks a minimum of three years and preferably as long as seven.* Retain contracts and deeds for life. Keep insurance policies until they have been canceled or cashed in. If you have borrowed against an insurance policy, keep the note for the loan with the policy.

Record keeping should remain as uncomplicated as possible. A simple budget, plan to spend, and monthly record of expenses due and paid is sufficient for most clergy families.

Putting financial records in order is essential. A little

organization will prove very beneficial for planning, record keeping, and preparing income tax forms. Some people use elaborate systems with log books and files or expensive computer software programs, but in my opinion these require more time and diligence to keep them up to date.

The old "envelope" system is simple but still works. Large manila envelopes should be marked for major categories. Place receipts, charge slips, and canceled checks— anything that has a tax or budget consequence—in the appropriate envelope. Survey the contents of each envelope quarterly and clean it out annually.

The same kind of envelope system may work effectively for cash outlays over the month, such as the "food and staple" money, children's allowances, or payment to the newspaper carrier. Most items in a budget will be and should be paid by check, but candidates for an envelope would be those cash items that recur each week or month. The point is to put them aside and avoid commingling, which raises a temptation to spend outside the budgeted areas.

BUDGET CATEGORIES

The major categories of the clergy budget are as follows:

Tithe/Offerings

It is my firm opinion that all clergy must consider a tithe or proportionate giving. The offering is anything on top of this amount. A pastor must model this kind of giving for the congregation he leads. This is biblically demanded.

It is not easy to allocate $1,500 of a $15,000 salary for God's work, but it is a correct biblical response that honors God. It was difficult for us to tithe in the early years of our ministry, but it was essential that we initiate good tithing habits at that time.

I believe a pastor's tithe should be returned to the church the pastor is serving. My reasons are that, first, the tithe should be returned to the congregation out of loyalty to the source of the income. Second, although few will know of your tithing to the local church, it will establish your credibility as one who believes in the church enough to support it fully. Third, the local church is the institution that ministers directly to me and my family. It is not inconsistent to practice "storehouse" tithing—that is, the church should receive the tithe, and any giving to other organizations and ministries should come from funds over and above that 10 percent.

The "offering" may well go to support alumni institutions, missionary friends, radio and television ministries, or parachurch ministries.

Tithes and offerings must have first priority in the budget. The spiritual dimension must be primary, and the clergy family that is inadequate in this part of the budget harms itself and its ministry.

Savings/Investments

Many clergy participate in a church or denominational retirement plan. A minimum guideline is to save 10 percent of net income per year. Whatever contribution might be made by the church or denomination itself should be included in the 10 percent. But do not include home equity appreciation as savings, since that amount fluctuates and is not cash. Since 10 percent is the minimum standard, it is worth seeking to match the church contribution out of your personal income. The pastor who exceeds 10 percent in savings early in his career will profit in retirement, especially since savings may double every seven to ten years.

Food/Household

The cost of family food and household expenses entails many variables such as size of family, geographic location, opportunity to grow or receive farm products, and eating habits. See the next chapter for some cost-cutting suggestions in shopping for groceries.

Clothing

Clothing is a budget item that may vary widely among clergy. The pastor and his family must be presentable. Yet families with small, growing children may find clothing to require a disproportionate share of the budget, even though sales are common enough to provide considerable savings. You as the minister will probably need to purchase a new suit every year or so. Some parishioners can be very helpful. I know of one pastor who is told to visit a men's store each year and choose a dress suit, all at the expense of this thoughtful member of his congregation. But not all are so blessed. So the clothing budget needs careful, preseason planning.

See the next chapter for some money-saving suggestions, especially in regard to used clothing.

Transportation

Owning a car is a major expense in any budget. The cost of transportation must include parking fees and tolls as well as auto maintenance. Hertz Company recently estimated the cost of operating a compact car at $4,800 per year.

Auto leasing has become an option. A lease does not require a down payment and may run three to four years. The lease payments are usually smaller than car payments and are tax deductible. One disadvantage is that after the lease expires, there is no equity. Another is that some lease arrangements penalize the lessee if the car is driven more than 15,000 miles per year. This is an option for families with good credit but no funds for making a purchase. It is also a choice for clergy using a car as a business expense.

An essential tool for record keeping is a simple notebook or log kept in the car to record expenses and mileage. We will need this if we will deduct auto expenses for tax purposes. Log all business miles.

Taxes

State and federal taxes affect most clergy families quarterly. Since most clergy are considered by the Internal Revenue Service to be self-employed, they must pay an estimated income tax and the social security tax by the fifteenth day of April, June, September, and January. (They are considered quarterly even though they do not fall exactly every three months.) Even clergy without sufficient income to have federal tax liability must, unless it is waived previously, pay the social security tax quarterly.

Many clergy do not anticipate these dates and therefore find themselves short hundreds of dollars and end up with short-term borrowing. This begins to dig a financial hole that is difficult to climb out of.

These quarterly payments should be figured into the monthly budget so that the cash is available when the payments come due. It has been the practice in my family to write a monthly check to ourselves for that amount. Quarterly we void the checks and write the amount back in the checkbook balance, then write out the check for the IRS. Others may want to place such money in savings, and then use it quarterly. A NOW (negotiable order of withdrawal) checking account accomplishes both goals.

Property taxes for home owners are best held in escrow and thus should be figured into the monthly mortgage payment. If not held in escrow, these funds should be kept in a savings account established specifically for a tax fund. The fact is, it is far better to set aside the money for taxes and thereby earn interest, if the bank allows us to do so and we are able to discipline ourselves to do it.

Housing

Few clergy rent. Most either own their own homes or live in a parsonage/manse provided by the church. Whatever the case, this item is normally the largest in the budget. If a manse is provided, the clergy do not need to budget housing costs, but the value of that housing—which is not always easily calculated and varies according to geographical location—is excluded from the financial package. An alternative is for the clergy to provide for their own housing and receive a housing allowance in their package.

Insurance

Health, life, disability, auto—these and more will be a part of the clergy budget. Chapter 7 suggests the best insurance planning. In terms of the budget, most clergy either overspend or poorly allocate insurance dollars. An annual insurance review is essential to good planning.

Celebrations

No one wants to neglect pleasurable occasions such as birthdays, anniversaries, and weddings. Gifts are important and should be included in the budget. Why not set a monetary limit for birthdays and holidays? Be creative and make gifts instead of purchasing them, where this is practical. Moreover, a card with a personal thought is probably appreciated as much as an expensive gift.

Giving gifts at a wedding is a touchy issue for clergy. In one pastorate I averaged more than forty weddings per year! My wife and I gave a standard gift to all couples—a devotional book to be used in the first year of marriage. Inexpensive, yes, but it may have encouraged some lasting devotional habits. It did not hurt our budget, and giving the same gift to all avoided showing favoritism.

Entertainment/Relaxation

We all need times of rest and relaxation, but budget restraints may become a hindrance. Vacation, hobby, and entertainment needs must be planned. Some clergy have access to the vacation homes of parishioners at no cost, and this is a significant budget saver.

Professional Expenses

Items that can be included under "professional expenses" cover a wide range: books, educational costs, past educational debt, annual professional fees. It is all too easy to break the budget on these kinds of items. A growing and serious problem is past educational debt; seminarians today accumulate as much as $20,000 debt that must be repaid within ten years of graduation.

Safety Deposit Box

Every family should consider leasing a small safety deposit box at the same place it does its banking or another financial institution near home. The cost will range from $20 to $40 a year.

The box should contain insurance policies (or at least a list of policy numbers), coin collections, property deeds, car title, and any other papers that might have legal significance. The older you become, the more material the box will contain. Both spouses should have access to it.

A variety of budget planning books are available at office supply stores or bookstores. A traditional model is *The Consumer's Almanac,* a diary of spending and income that also offers advice and consumer information. One feature, for example, is the "shopping bag," which lists good buys for each month and season. It can be purchased from the American Financial Association in Washington, D.C.

Diligent record keeping and budgeting can be tedious. But few clergy will attain financial stability without these disciplines. The alternative is fiscal mismanagement. The method of budgeting and record keeping we may choose is secondary and optional. What is important is that we do it and do it satisfactorily.

6 | *HOW TO LIVE ON LESS AS CLERGY*

Clergy salaries have never been considered career motivating. Each of us knows that our "call to ministry" did not include financial security. For most it has proved to be continuing financial jeopardy.

A church board was recently shocked when it discovered the pastor's wife was using government food stamps. Embarrassed, the congregation immediately raised the pastor's salary.

Yet compensation is appreciably better than it was just a generation ago. This is certainly due in part to the laity's greater awareness of clergy needs. Another factor, especially in evangelical and fundamentalist circles, is the trend toward larger congregations. Although church membership still averages in the seventies, according to Lyle Schaller, a church growth authority, the proportion of larger churches has risen and with that have come higher salaries. It is not uncommon to find evangelical pastors in a metropolitan-suburban area receiving more than $30,000 in cash plus benefits.

Graduates from Trinity Evangelical Divinity School are now receiving on average about $17,500 including cash and benefits as they enter their first full-time positions.

The negative side is that the vast majority of clergy are still in smaller, low-salaried churches. In increasing numbers they rely on the second income of a working spouse to make ends meet. Some clergy also hold part-time, "moonlighting" jobs with the consent of the church officers.

Churches must come to grips with the salary question. Minimum salaries should be established in every denomination.

Until these economic conditions improve, it is expedient that clergy find ways to stretch their dollars and "live on less." But how? It begins with good budgeting. The family is forced to examine priorities in spending. In that regard, let us look at some areas of concern.

THE CASH/CREDIT DILEMMA

Cash is generally preferred as the way to obtain what we need. Debt can be harmful if it is used in the wrong way or for the wrong purchase. Some items necessarily are financed by credit, including home, car, major appliances, and part of college expenses.

Debt may be disabling to the less disciplined. The "credit card syndrome" can strike clergy as easily as it can laypeople and in some cases has wrought financial disaster. Money problems, often produced by indebtedness, have caused many resignations from ministry and have raised marital and family stress to the breaking point.

How should you use credit? These guidelines will help keep credit matters under control:

1. *Look for the best rate among the national credit cards.* A variety of rates and annual charges are offered by lending institutions. The bank need not be in your town or state. Besides the interest rate, check for any annual fees and the date of monthly billing. The three items to check are (a) the rate, (b) the annual fee, and (c) the date of monthly billing (some companies bill from date of purchase).

2. *Limit yourself to one major national card.* Few need more than one among Visa, Mastercard, Diners, Discovery, and American Express. Credit card companies or lending institutions will often send cards without request. Tear them up: having them may build your ego, but they will also build

your debt. Note that Diners and American Express must be paid in full each month.

3. *Determine a limit on what you can afford in credit cards.* What will the budget allow? Once that is determined, keep the total indebtedness of all cards—national, department store, and/or gasoline—within those limits.

4. *Use credit for the right purchases.* Never use a credit card for food and staples. Purchase major items with credit, but always with a plan to pay off the debt as soon as possible. Using credit cards to finance vacations is risky because the financial consequences may sour a good experience.

5. *Pay off all credit within thirty days if possible.* This avoids your paying interest. Department store credit in particular should be treated as a thirty-day account.

6. *Always check the terms of your credit.* Many credit companies charge interest from the date of purchase; this increases the cost of credit.

7. *Figure your interest into the cost of the purchase.* If a refrigerator costs $600 and you will make payments over twelve months at 20 percent interest, you must realize that the real cost of the appliance is $720. You may still make the purchase, but recognizing the cost of credit may motivate you to save up the cash first or make a larger down payment.

8. *Save for planned purchases, and use credit for emergency buying.* The refrigerator is a case in point. If you desire to replace it next year, then save all or some of the funds needed. If the refrigerator suddenly breaks down and cannot be repaired, then use a credit card for an immediate purchase if the cash is not at hand.

IMPULSE BUYING

Many clergy are prone to impulse buying. Why? They are very likely to spend some of their time on a day off at a shopping mall.

Impulse buying at the grocery store is the easiest to

handle. One person should do the shopping with a prepared list. Children as shopping companions often encourage impulse buying. In our family my wife does the shopping, and she goes alone because she is less inclined than I toward buying on impulse.

The problem appears not only in the supermarket or mall, but for some clergy, at the bookstore. I am always ready to rationalize my book purchases. I disciplined this urge to overspend on books by purchasing only those that had been reviewed in publications such as *Christianity Today* and *Eternity*. This rule stalled some impulse book purchases. Another money-saver was a plan I instituted early in my ministry. I simply asked the congregation to share magazines they had read. I received *Newsweek, Time, U.S. News & World Report, Fortune,* and *Business Week,* among others, often from only two days to a week after parishioners had received and read them. One parishioner gave me a week's worth of the *Wall Street Journal* every Sunday; finally my friend decided it was simpler just to order a subscription of the *Journal* for me, and this continued during the entire time I served that church.

I have no doubt I was the best-read pastor in town— without spending a penny. In fact, the publications I regularly received from church members, not counting the *Journal,* would have cost me more than $400 in subscriptions. All that was needed was an announcement in the bulletin, and the magazines came in a steady flow.

DISCOUNTS AND COUPONS

Clergy have gained a reputation as notorious discount hunters. In smaller communities, businesses often offer a clergy discount. I believe one should never ask for a discount, but naturally use one if it is offered. The profession need not be demeaned. Clergy tend to learn when and where discounts are available, and the local ministerial association shares the news.

Coupons may be offered in magazines and newspapers. Some people almost make a fetish of collecting them, but be sure they actually save you money over against another product of equal quality. And do not buy hordes of supplies or food that will not soon be used. Coupons may provide valid savings within the limits of common sense.

FOOD AND HOUSEHOLD EXPENSES

There are many ways to economize with the food budget. We do well to keep these observations in mind regarding grocery shopping:

1. Two people shopping together at a supermarket are likely to spend more than one person doing the shopping alone. This is the result of two extra eyes and nostrils—all the senses—and the tendency toward impulse buying.

2. Having a written shopping list reduces impulse buying. The smart shopper also shops with a hand calculator to add up the cost of the food basket, but also to figure the best buys per ounce. Some large stores note the price per ounce or pound for every item on shelf price tags.

3. "Convenience" or "fast food" meals must be included in a food budget. A night at McDonald's or a late-night pizza must be calculated as a food cost.

4. Shop once a week or once a paycheck for major shopping needs, with basic menus planned. This helps avoid stops in between times at convenience stores, which often charge higher prices.

5. Have enough cash on hand for weekly needs such as school lunches, allowances, intermediate food shopping, and an occasional fast food meal. Remember to list this incidental cash in the budget book along with the large weekly checks and expenditures.

CLOTHING

Clergy have often been the recipients of good—sometimes excellent—used clothing. Secondhand items for young and preteen children can be especially useful because they are often outgrown well before the original owners have worn them out. Don't be embarrassed or shy about accepting such goods from friends.

Some families frequent used-clothing stores, but be careful that the cost-cutting does not leave you and your family wearing wide lapels that are five years out of style. Use discernment in choosing between style and savings.

Blessed are garage sales! One of my daughters-in-law, a pastor's wife, has saved many dollars at garage sales; when her family has outgrown the clothes, she offers them at her own sale. (Toys, games, and sports equipment are other items that can be bought as bargains at garage sales.)

Establish your own "layaway" plan by setting aside small amounts regularly for anticipated clothing needs that are not likely to be met at the secondhand store.

VACATIONS AND "GETAWAYS"

What do you do when you "need a break" from the routine? Vacations cost money, but there are economical options available to clergy. Sometimes someone in the church will make a second home or vacation cottage available to the clergy and his family for a week or two. By this means we have been able to enjoy family vacations in Minnesota, Michigan, Wisconsin, Florida, Colorado, and Arizona without the great expense of accommodations. Some clergy are surprised at how pleased the owners are to lend their homes. It is important to clean the home or cottage thoroughly before leaving and to send a homemade gift or flowers afterward in appreciation for the kindness.

Children cherish vacations and occasional, brief getaways as much as adults. These times have provided fond family memories at minimal expense.

CONCLUSION

The main purpose of this chapter is not to enumerate a variety of economizing measures in many categories.

Rather, it is to challenge the clergy family to be as creative as possible in its use of money. The demands of the profession, in large churches or small, often entail added or unforeseen expenses, but these are frequently offset by some financial advantages unavailable to others.

Living on less is both a necessity and an example of good stewardship for most clergy. For many it may be a question of financial survival. Moonlighting will always be difficult and dissipate the time, interest, and energy that should be devoted to the needs of the congregation.

Underpaid clergy are subject to both mental and spiritual stress. The families in the congregation, and especially the leadership, often have lifestyles appreciably better than the pastor's. The struggle comes in realizing that the pastor has had seven years or more of higher education, accumulating years of experience besides, yet is compelled not just to "live on less," but to find ways to survive financially. This problem must be faced honestly lest it cause clergy to forsake their calling and ministry. It requires deeper motivation. Ministry has rewards, but seldom are they financial.

7 | THE GREAT INSURANCE QUESTION

Clergy are often anxious about insurance, especially life insurance. This may be due to the fact that we deal so often with death and dying, and we have indelible memories of widows left without necessary provision. Physicians and funeral directors seem to face the same dilemma.

How long we live obviously influences our answer to the question, How should I provide for my family in the event of my death? If death came in one's forties, the needs would be sharply escalated compared with the death of a seventy-year-old.

Life insurance is important, and there is no monetary substitute for it. Our dependents need our financial care. Life insurance, unless we have a living financial estate, is the vehicle to care for dependents.

The purpose of financial planning is to produce a living estate in line with our financial goals. Therefore, our life insurance needs will change with our financial status. In other words, every clergy must desire to be self-insured eventually, hopefully by the time of retirement.

Each clergy family must view life insurance as a financial umbrella to cover the time of need. Life insurance buys time to accumulate an estate. It is humorous but sad that many older clergy have large insurance policies to protect nonexistent dependents. One friend was still carrying some $300,000 of insurance at retirement. His children were in their forties, and his wife had died four years earlier!

His only justification would be to leave an estate for his children, but the insurance premiums were cramping his present lifestyle and making him dependent on others. In fact, his children did not need his estate; they were much more concerned about his present welfare.

Keep in mind that the purpose of life insurance is to cover our financial need over a specific period of time. So we must annually review our net worth and with it our financial goals, but especially insurance needs. Policies can be changed, dropped, or even purchased from another company. Insurance plans should never be static.

TYPES OF INSURANCE COMPANIES

There are two basic types of insurance companies. They are designated as "par" and "nonpar," or participating and nonparticipating.

Nonparticipating plans are sold by companies that are owned by stockholders, and the profits or losses are shared by the stockholders.

Participating policies are sold by firms that are often described as a "mutual." The selling point is that the "par" policy allows us a return in the form of "dividends" on our policy premium.

The truth is that we receive a return on an overcharge, not a dividend! Moreover, there is never a guarantee that the policy will return anything. The next time a salesperson seeks to sell a policy on the basis of "the dividend return," ask the question, "Then why is my dividend not taxed by the Internal Revenue Service?" The answer is simply that the "dividend" is a return of an overcharge.

The test of whether a "dividend" is truly a dividend or instead a return on overcharge is its liability to tax. If it is not taxed, it is an overcharge. This overcharge can range from 16 to 44 percent of the annual premium. That is costly participation, but it sounds good to be told that we may receive a dividend of up to 44 percent return at year's end.

A good course of action is to compare the cost of the same policy par and nonpar. Usually you will find that the nonpar policy premiums are lower. (The lower lefthand side of the policy will identify par or nonpar.) The other problem with the "participating" policy is that the insurance company holds the overcharge, uses it, and makes the decision of how much and when you get the overcharge back!

TYPES OF LIFE INSURANCE POLICIES

There are two basic types of life insurance—"term" and "whole life"—but many varieties within the two groups. The new "universal" policies are really a combination of both term and whole life.

Term Insurance

"Term" is protection alone, with no provision for savings. We insure our lives against the "accident" of death. This policy is a simple agreement, with nothing complicated, no cash value, no savings. It is like car insurance: we use it only in case of accident! It is an essential part of the financial umbrella over the family. Many insurance agents will try to sell us anything but term insurance because the commissions are not large and the company doesn't profit as much as with a whole life policy. Also, most term insurance policies should be canceled when our living estate has passed a term policy need.

Term insurance will always carry the lower premiums. The argument is that if we cancel at sixty or sixty-five we have received nothing. But we have—protection in case of death! We didn't buy the policy to build an estate; we bought it for protection.

There are three basic kinds of term insurance: renewable, decreasing, or level. The renewable is usually provided on an annualized basis. This term policy has either a guaranteed rate or a current rate. The guaranteed rate will always be a bit higher due to the risk the company takes regarding future economic conditions. The rate will change each year or every few years based on current conditions.

It is wise to ask an agent for a summary of the rates over the last ten years. This will indicate whether a policy that begins with a low rate is likely to rise in the future. The least expensive of these policies is purchased through a group plan, such as credit card members, denominational associations, or the like. Check whether the policy is automatically canceled upon leaving the group.

Decreasing term is another type of term insurance. It is familiar as a policy offered to home owners for mortgages, and to car owners to cover future payments. This kind of insurance has been called mortgage insurance, but it is really a decreasing term insurance policy, offered to cover the debt. It is so-called because the rate of coverage decreases with the amortization schedule of the loan. Essentially, the amount of the debt is covered at any given time and no more. Never assume the insurance offered by the lending institution is the best buy; shop around for it.

This form of term is not just an option for major purchases. It may be a part of your total insurance package. For instance, I calculated my three children would be in college over nine years. I purchased a ten-year decreasing term policy that would have covered a major portion of their college costs during that period had I died. After seven years, I canceled the policy. The cost for this protection was about $5 per month. It was protection for a period of time, not an investment. This decreasing term policy gave me peace of mind in regard to educating my children at a low cost.

Decreasing term can also be used to cover a period of time when a wife is outside the umbrella of social security protection, as when the last child has departed the home and before retirement benefits begin. This is usually the time from ages forty-five to sixty-two.

The third kind of term insurance is level term. The premium remains level for a predetermined time, usually five years, and then a new rate is set for another period of years. Level term is simply cost averaging, and we must realize that we are overpaying in the early years and underpaying in later years. Therefore, level term policies should have a fixed length of time, perhaps twenty or thirty years; canceling out early is not fiscally responsible.

Term insurance should be the major component in your

insurance program. In fact, I hold that it should be our only type of life insurance type until we reach the fifties, when consideration could be given to a variable universal life policy, which we will discuss later.

Whole Life Insurance

The second major type of insurance is whole life. This policy seeks to combine protection and savings. Therefore the premium will be much higher in relation to the dollar amount of the protection. This policy has a face amount and premium staying the same for the life of the policyholder. Again, the mortality chart is consulted, the company's risk is calculated, and a constant premium rate is determined. Again, we are basically overpaying in earlier years so that the premiums later on will not be inordinately high.

The question this raises is, why should we build our savings through an insurance company, without the flexibility and liquidity of other instruments? The only sensible answer is that we may not have the discipline to save any other way; it forces us to save. But we pay a high price for our lack of discipline. It is better to buy term insurance and invest the difference in the cost of the premiums ourselves. Poor planning and buying of insurance has strapped many clergy families. Agents can exploit our weakness in not wanting to leave the family destitute, and the lower the income the greater the fear factor.

All rates are based on mortality tables plus expense and profit for the company. Since each year brings us closer to the day we die, premiums increase. Even "level" premiums are devised by averaging out the company's cost over twenty years. This is much like a budget plan for utilities: the annual bill is divided into equal payments, even though the actual cost of the energy we consume varies from month to month. Level insurance takes the "life bill" and divides it into equal, or level, annual or semi-annual payments.

Most whole life policies reach the break-even level when the policyholder is about age sixty-three to sixty-five. Assume a male life expectancy of seventy-seven years, and if we purchased the whole policy at age twenty-five, we would have overpaid for close to forty years and underpaid for less then fifteen years! Does this make sense?

Insurance agents rightfully claim that a portion of those early premiums are applied to "cash surrender." But be aware that our estate does not get the face amount plus cash surrender. Rather, that's the amount we receive if we cancel. Look at it another way: the longer the policy is in effect, the less financial liability there is for the insurance company.

Another factor is that we can borrow against our policy up to its cash value. But upon our death, this amount will be deducted from the face value of the policy. Yes, the interest we pay to borrow that money will generally be lower than a bank will charge, but all we are really doing is borrowing our own money and paying to do it!

There are only two ways to get the cash value: either die, or borrow against it and pay the company interest. It is not considered our money; it is theirs, and eventually it comes out of our estate. Of course, you can get the cash value back by surrendering the policy in a cancellation of coverage.

I repeat: only term insurance kept until death is permanent insurance protection at a reasonable cost.

Endowment Insurance

My first child was born in 1955 and entered college in 1973. I distinctly remember an insurance agent in my first pastorate visiting me at the office, offering me the best deal ever: I should buy a $10,000, twenty-year endowment policy so that my new son could have his years of college funded. The premium was difficult to pay on a very limited salary, and I had just purchased a term life policy. I declined. The words of the agent still ring in my ears: "You'll be sorry! Remember $10,000 in twenty years." The policy would have cost me more than $7,000 in premiums over twenty years—and my return was to be only $10,000.

Now even if I could have afforded his "endowment policy," I should have declined and put the money each month into a mutual fund. By investing even in a conservative mutual fund on the same payment basis as the endowment policy, I would have seen my earnings on $7,000 grow to $17,000. That is 70 percent better then the "great deal" offered in the endowment policy.

The premiums on endowment insurance are high because the company must earn back a certain amount over a shorter period of time.

Endowment policies are really out-of-fashion today. Annuities and universal variables offer a much better option, but I still meet clergy who have been talked into funding a college education for their children with an endowment policy. I recommend building savings some other way.

Universal Life Policies

Recent additions to the life insurance menu have been called "universal life," and they now have the offshoots "universal variable life" and "single premium life."

I suspect that insurance companies were forced to market a better policy than whole life due to the pressure of financial advisers like Venita Van Caspel, author of *Money Dynamics* (New York: Simon and Schuster, 1974). Van Caspel titled chapter 13 "Life Insurance—The Great National Consumer Fraud." More than four million copies of that chapter were distributed. In my opinion, "universal life" policies were created as a response to this criticism.

A revised edition of Van Caspel's book, entitled *Money Dynamics for the New Economy* (Reston, Va.: Reston Publishing, 1980), also devotes chapter 13 to insurance, but calls it "Life Insurance—Still the Great National Consumer Dilemma."

Besides term insurance, Van Caspel recommends universal variable life insurance. Universal life begins with a determined death benefit and premium, but allows us to exercise some flexibility. The policy is divided into three segments: life protection, savings, and expense. In variable universal, the cash we accrue is placed in a mutual fund rather than a general account. This allows us to choose our investment instrument between government bonds, equity stocks, or a money market account. We may move our money, usually for a fee, from one account to another.

The advantage of universal policies is that they offer investment opportunities with life insurance. Most allow the insured to control the investment decisions. And the policy has loan potential. The disadvantage is that these policies demand a large single premium or an annual amount higher than clergy budgets allow. These policies generally are better than whole, ordinary, or endowment insurance—in part, probably, because of critiques by people like Van Caspel.

As you read the prospectus for a universal life policy, be alert for three things. First, make sure you are buying a variable policy; second, be concerned about the options of investment from equity to secure government bonds; and third, make sure the prospectus does not allow for the insurance company to make the investment decisions. You should be empowered to make them if you choose to do so.

Another outstanding feature of this policy is that any accumulation is tax-deferred. I do not see this as an alternative to a denominational retirement plan, but it could be an interesting option for mature clergy looking for protection and investment.

MAKING DECISIONS ABOUT LIFE INSURANCE

How much life insurance to purchase is always a difficult decision, but basically the question can be answered with a formula that begins with the assumption that a family with children will need an amount equal to 75 to 80 percent of the current income. A childless couple or one with grown children would probably require an amount equal to about 60 percent of income.

Let's consider "Karl." The total income for Karl's family is about $30,000 per year. Karl has three children, all under eighteen. His wife "Karen" is a substitute teacher who contributes about 10 percent of the $30,000.

In order for Karen to live at a level of 80 percent of the family income, the total investments (including social security) must produce about $24,000 annually. The following chart calculates the minimum insurance need.

$24,000	Annual goal
3,000	Karen's part-time employment
11,000	Social security benefits (depending on status of children)
1,500	Present investment earnings (retirement plan)
$15,500	Total realized
$8,500	Net amount needed to be supplied by insurance

Based on a 7 percent return on investment, and not factoring in the effects of inflation, Karl must carry a minimum of $125,000 of insurance. But he must adjust these figures every year or so to account for inflation, a higher family budget, raises, and greater anticipated earnings from the retirement plan. Insurance should be evaluated annually.

Another formula is simply to insure ourselves at four or five times our annual salary. This should provide for our family's minimum financial needs in the event of our death.

Insuring Your Spouse and Children

The question of whether to insure dependents is one I am often asked in financial seminars. Let me deal first with children. Do they produce income for the family? No. Therefore, why insure them, precious as they may be?

Life insurance for children should only cover burial costs, and this can often be added as a rider to our policy. If a rider is not available, forget the matter altogether.

Insuring a wife, however, is a different matter. Look at it this way: (1) how much does my wife contribute to our family income? (2) how much would child care and related expenses cost me if she died? The answer to these questions determines the amount of insurance needed.

If you desire some insurance coverage for your mate, I suggest a declining or level term policy over the fifteen years or so of preteen and teenage family growth. That will be sufficient. This is one kind of insurance I passed up, and neither my wife nor I ever had qualms concerning it. The potential cost of child care is prohibitive if you are covering this in your mate's life insurance. We took the risk of not providing for it.

Double Indemnity and Accident Policies

Indemnities, double or triple, are paid off in the event of accidental death. Check the statistics relating to accidental deaths, and you will immediately realize that the odds of ever cashing in such a policy are very low.

Some credit card companies offer an accidental death policy without apparent charge as a marketing device. If it doesn't cost anything, take it, but look for hidden costs.

My advice is to take a pass on all forms of accidental death policies. You would be better served to spend the money on some good books!

Disability Insurance

Disability coverage is one of the most neglected segments of a clergy insurance package. Statistics suggest that more than 20 percent of professional people suffer some period of disability at some time during their lives.

There are some questions we must ask before shopping for disability insurance.

First, how much should we have? We can usually get insurance to cover us up to 60 percent of our gross income.

Second, when do we want the insurance to start? Policies can be written with an effective date of thirty days after the disability, or longer. The more risk we assume, the lower the premium. Normally a pastor's church will cover the first six months to a year of disability. I suggest a six-month waiting period as being most acceptable.

Third, how long should the policy be in effect? Most policies mature at age sixty-five or when full social security benefits are applicable.

Check carefully the following aspects of a disability policy: How is disability defined? Is disability determined by our ability to fulfill our profession? Consider the terms of renewability. The best policy is "noncancelable" and "guaranteed renewable." One must also check whether the policy pays in addition to social security disability or combines with social security to arrive at the disability amount. Ask whether you can enter a rehabilitation program without penalty. Does the policy cover previous illness?

These are just some of the questions that must be asked in regard to disability insurance. Normally this would be a church expense and should cost about $150 to $500 per year. If I were a member of a church board I would not want to neglect this coverage.

PROFESSIONAL LIABILITY INSURANCE

We live in a day of legal threats and suits. They are proliferating in every area of life. This problem also affects clergy. A generation ago, professional liability for clergy was unheard of. Today it would be unwise for a pastor to be without professional liability coverage.

A few prominent clergy or members of their staff have been sued over advice given during counseling. This is one problem area. The cost of this insurance is minimal, but the coverage gives counseling clergy a safety zone.

Check with your insurance agent for coverage. Shop around for it and make sure the agent provides a couple of cost quotes.

This is certainly an expense that should be assumed by the church or institution, but in any case it is coverage you will not want to neglect.

SUMMARY

Some guidelines may sum up this chapter on insurance.

1. Life insurance should be purchased for dying and not for investment. If we combine the two, we may lose both ways as regards the benefits.

2. Insurance programs should be reviewed annually. Our goal must be self-insurance. Any insurance is an umbrella to protect us until the time of self-insurance.

3. Mortality tables become the basis for all rates. The

last table was adopted in 1980. It is expected that life expectancy rates will be raised again when new tables are made. Always reexamine insurance costs after a new mortality table is adopted; your costs could be lower.

4. Invest wisely the difference in dollars between term premiums and whole life policies. The difference may amount to hundreds of dollars, even up to $2,000 per year. Let that money work for you by gaining interest.

5. Never buy an insurance policy that offers less then $100,000 in face value. The cost of smaller policies is usually expensive.

6. Clergy should never buy insurance from a church member or friend. Feelings arising from a sense of obligation to the agent can cloud good judgment.

7. Think twice before buying insurance coverage for a spouse unless she produces more than 30 percent of the family income. Shun individual policies on children.

8. Most clergy are able to save money by examining their insurance programs, often discovering an overpurchase of insurance or the purchase of an inappropriate policy.

9. Don't be afraid to cash in a whole life policy. It is wise to buy term to replace it and receive more coverage. Save the money you don't spend on the term policy.

10. Insurance is an emotional issue. Have enough to allow you to sleep; but do not become insurance poor. The best odds are that you will live into your seventies, and hopefully at that time you will be self-insured.

8 | A HOUSE IS MORE THAN A SHELTER

One of the most important decisions that clergy make is the matter of housing. Pastors find that their residences are likely to change more often than in any other profession. Doctors and lawyers build a practice for a lifetime and at most will relocate within the community from a smaller to a larger house due to family growth. A pastor will probably move four to six times during his career. This means that clergy face more risk, more potential gain or loss, and more changes in some furnishings, the size of home, the style of architecture, and all the other variables entailed in a relocation of residence. Add to this a change of location, often hundreds of miles away, and the complexities are compounded.

Yes, the matter of housing is a most important decision for clergy. A good career move can be jeopardized by selecting a home or occupying a parsonage that is viewed with disfavor by other members of the family. For instance, a child who has enjoyed a 10-by-12-foot bedroom finds that his room in the next parsonage is 9 by 10 feet—25 percent less space. What will a teenager think of that! Or a wife leaves a kitchen with more than adequate cabinets and work space for a home with meager work and storage areas. A family leaves a home on an acre of land and moves into a home on one-quarter acre. Suddenly a "closed-in" feeling has to be dealt with in the adjustment to a new residence.

Many pastoral moves are jeopardized or forsaken due,

first, to the change in houses and, second, the difference in location. The physical aspects of the parsonage and the desirability of the location are always major considerations in making a move.

Let's look carefully at the entire matter of housing for clergy. It is a matter not always understood even by the best-intentioned layperson.

ADVANTAGES OF OWNERSHIP

"To buy or not to buy" is the primary question that faces most clergy. Sometime during their lives they will encounter the question of living in a parsonage or purchasing a home. Few clergy rent a residence.

The growth of home ownership has been a phenomenon in the church scene in the United States over the past twenty-five years. The European model is still in the mode of the parsonage; few clergy own their own homes on the Continent. It has been estimated that in the United States more than 40 percent of all pastors now own their homes or have had the option to own, and the percentage is steadily increasing.

Why should you own a home? There are obvious advantages:

1. Equity (the difference between the purchase price and the market value at any given time) increases over time. But be careful in times of low inflation or deflation, for equity may be more a dream than a reality.

2. One has the opportunity to remodel, renovate, or redecorate without permission from church authorities. Freedom is an advantage of ownership.

3. The choice of location, size, and design of a home is guaranteed in ownership. Parsonages do not allow those choices; you will be locked into a situation that does not accommodate preferences.

4. The use of equity for other needs. One of the least-

known advantages to ownership is that of home equity loan possibilities.

Let us illustrate this with a pastor who purchased a home ten years ago and, through loan payments but especially through appreciation, has increased equity. His $60,000 home was purchased with a $50,000 mortgage ten years ago; $44,000 now remains on the principal. In ten years the value has appreciated 50 percent to $120,000. Most financial institutions will lend up to 80 percent of appraised value, so now the equity for loan has become approximately $50,000.

Note, however, that the clergyman's house payments, if he refinances, will double. The other side of this issue is that few would refinance an equity loan for the entire amount, but to refinance for less than $10,000 is probably too costly due to the closing costs and miscellaneous fees.

An additional factor is that the pastor has probably had salary increases accumulating to 50 percent in those ten years, while his house payments have remained constant. Therefore he may be quite capable of handling the equity loan payments.

5. There is a great tax advantage in ownership. A "double dip" for clergy is allowed: there is not only a benefit in a housing allowance (available to renters and parsonage residents), but also a tax deduction for interest paid on the mortgage.

DISADVANTAGES OF OWNERSHIP

One does encounter disadvantages with home ownership, however. These problems must be faced squarely.

1. Cash is needed for a down payment. Few clergy, especially those newly graduated from seminary, have the cash required for a down payment. Other clergy, after years of living in a parsonage, will often be just as strapped and lack the resources for the down payment, which is usually expected to be about 20 percent of the cost of the home.

Many churches have wisely contracted with the pastor

to provide a loan at either low interest or no interest. Some churches "forgive" this loan over the term of service as pastor. Note that this forgiven money must be treated as income; the amount forgiven in a particular year (whether at a steady rate or a graduated rate) must be declared as income on the tax return.

For example, suppose you were provided with a $20,000 loan, which is being remitted at the rate of $2,000 per year. The amount of $2,000 must be included as part of your adjusted gross income on your annual tax return.

2. The flexibility for future pastoral moves is hindered by home purchase. Home ownership has appreciably increased the length of tenure for pastors. The negative aspect of this is, ownership has caused some clergy to retain their pastorates longer than normal. In fact, some have jeopardized future ministry by remaining beyond the time when their relationship with a congregation should have ended. If parsonages had been provided, it would have been easier for the pastors to leave at the appropriate time.

A pastor occupying a parsonage has more flexibility than a home owner. He can make a decision regarding a call without the complication of selling a home or of separation from the family while waiting for a sale. This is the other side of "freedom." In this case it is freedom to make an unencumbered choice concerning a call to another church.

3. A third problem, not always apparent when one is trying to decide whether to own a home, is the matter of maintenance. Upkeep can entail great expense. There are bound to be unforeseen costs in making a new residence ready for occupancy. Often you will wish the church owned the home, especially when the furnace breaks down and the roof needs replacing! Maintenance costs escalate with the age of the home.

We must realize that many clergy will not have the opportunity to choose between ownership or the use of a parsonage. Yet one wishes every clergyman would have an opportunity, at some stage in his career, to build equity. If parsonage use is the only option offered to us, we must try as best as we can to begin a "home fund"—a special monthly investment in a growth mutual fund that will enable us at retirement to have resources to purchase that first home!

Missionaries often purchase a home in their hometown. A friend will kindly "watch care" over the property and rent out the home to cover mortgage payments and maintenance expenses. Years later, a home is available or equity has accumulated for retirement.

I personally would discourage ownership in rural, depressed, or overdeveloped areas. It is better to use a parsonage or rent a house and seek to save for future investment. Nor would I purchase if it is likely that my tenure in the position is going to be less than five years; the cost and risks of being caught at a disadvantage are too great. Third, and most important, I would not buy a home during my first year in a pastorate. This condition might well cause a hardship in that it requires a second move soon after the first; but if a family has rented for about a year, it is more knowledgeable to make a satisfying decision regarding the cost of a home and its location. Of course, it is not always possible to delay the decision of home purchase a whole year.

Let us assume that we have made the choice to purchase or build a home. Costs will vary in each area (see end of chapter).

FINANCING THE HOME

The first step in financing a home purchase is to provide for a down payment. Loans guaranteed by the Federal Housing Authority (FHA) can be obtained for as little as 5 percent down to those who qualify. Conventional loans generally demand a down payment of 20 percent. This money must come from personal savings, a family loan, a gift, or a church-provided loan. But there are usually restrictions on the kinds of loans a mortgagor will allow in obtaining a down payment, since a mortgage is itself a loan.

The average home sale price in the United States is now approaching $70,000. This means down payments will run, on the average, from $3,500 (FHA) to $14,000 (conventional mortgage). Of course, the higher the down payment, the better the possibility of obtaining a lower rate of interest on the mortgage.

The second matter we will face at most lending institutions is the auxiliary costs. These items include a fee for application that generally ranges from $100 to $300. This is merely a fee to cover the cost of an institution's work in providing a mortgage loan that they believe will earn money for them over the life of the contract. The loan officer will justify it by stating that the fee keeps indiscriminate and frivolous applications from proliferating, but if so, why not make it a deposit instead of a fee? All financial institutions levy this fee, and it must be paid to begin the process.

The next auxiliary costs will be a number of filing fees. One is an appraisal fee. This is the work of a qualified appraiser, and the cost will range from $100 to $200.

A "loan origination and discount fee" may also be charged, and this will be noted under "items payable in connection with the loan." These are commonly called "points." A loan may be granted at 10 percent plus two points. This fee means additional earnings for the lending institution. Points are always equated as a percentage of the loan; two points means simply 2 percent of the money borrowed, not 2 percent of the cost of the home. We note that points fluctuate with the percentage rate of interest. The lower the interest rate, the higher the points. The truth is, the institution will receive the same amount over the length of the contract. The lending institution always ends up with the same amount. This condition is built into every loan.

The decision on interest rates and points will probably be made on how much cash we have available. A higher interest rate will mean a lower cash outlay at the closing of the loan.

Some institutions will add a "commitment fee," usually below one hundred dollars. This is justified as a fee for making a commitment or promising the loan. Remember, when we borrow money for a home, we pay the lender for his privilege of making money on the loan!

Another charge will be title changes, which include such items as "title search" (about $150 to $300), "title examination" on purchase of a used home (normally under $200), and "title insurance," a fee that ensures that our title to the home is valid. This protection is essential, especially on an older home that has possibly had liens put on it by other lenders in past days; it is inadvisable on a new home.

"Government recording and transfer charges" is another category. This is the charge for "stamps," which can include local and state stamps, or taxes; they range from $50 to $150 in most areas. A recording fee is another government requirement. This is for recording the deed in the county office. The cost is usually less than $50.

Additional settlement charges may include a survey, a pest inspection in certain geographic areas, and plat drawings. These fees will vary from $15 to $200 or more.

Two other charges are becoming more prevalent. One is distinctive to an FHA loan. This is a prepaid mortgage insurance premium that will cover the entire life of the loan. The Federal Housing Authority guarantees the loan to the lender in case of our default, but we must pay for the insurance. The premium on a $75,000 mortgage will cost more than $2,500. It must be paid up front, no matter what kind of a credit rating we have, no matter how long the term of the loan. This premium is a major part of the closing cost entailed in an FHA loan. The offsetting factor is that the FHA usually demands a smaller down payment than a conventional mortgagor.

A second variable is "prepaid real estate tax." Many lenders will demand a one-year prepayment that is placed in escrow (set aside) in the borrower's name. This ensures that the taxes will be paid on time by the lender out of this account. We will be paying, in effect, one-twelfth of the annual tax with each monthly loan payment. The lender will review the escrow account annually to make sure we are depositing enough into it to cover any tax increases.

The alternative, the one that I prefer, is to pay one's

own real estate taxes out of pocket. Taxes are usually paid on a semi-annual basis; so invest the monthly payment and earn a few dollars' interest before taxes come due.

Let us recapitulate the major closing costs. These are paid in cash along with the agreed down payment.

Purchase price	$85,000
Down payment	10,000
Mortgage	75,000
Closing fees and charges	
Application fee	$150
Loan discount or "points," 2% of mortgage	1,500
Credit search	100
Mortgage insurance (FHA)	2,600
Prepaid homeowners insurance	220
Title fee search	250
Title insurance	175
Recording fees	25
State tax/stamps	120
Survey	150
Plat, name, special search	75
Total cash closing charges	$5,365

All these charges will be listed by the title company on a sheet called the "settlement statement." Ask for a dollar estimate before purchasing any home.

We see, therefore, from this accounting that the model FHA loan will cost our pastor $10,000 in down payment plus $5,365 in closing costs. Note that the down payment is only about 60 percent of the total cash cost at closing. Deduct $2,600 of mortgage insurance if a conventional loan is used; but increase the down payment from 15 percent to a minimum 20 percent, or an additional $5,000.

So our model pastor must plan on having available cash of about $15,000 to $18,000 to buy an $85,000 home.

The housing allowance is discussed in chapter 4. It is worth mentioning here, however, that the allowance offers a benefit to ordained and licensed clergy. The Tax Reform Act of 1986 lets clergy continue to exclude an allowance from earnings plus apply certain expenses to deductions.

HOW MUCH HOME CAN I AFFORD?

The question of what I can afford is really the basic issue. A credit search will always be made, and we should ask the lending institution for a personal copy. This will ensure that the credit bureau has up-to-date records and has not made mistakes; any errors or inadequate information must be corrected. Remember, we ourselves are paying for the credit search.

Most loan officers will figure the total family income and then lend up to 80 percent of the appraised value, if the payments do not exceed 30 to 33 percent of the family income. Some lending institutions may disregard a wife's earnings, especially when she is of child-bearing age.

The church treasurer will be asked to verify salary. Always use the gross figure, not the net figure reported to IRS. You need the higher figure to qualify for the loan. Many lending institutions will ask for the latest IRS Form 1040 filing, because of the self-employed status. I would seek to persuade the lender that verification from the church treasurer is sufficient.

It is wise never to assume mortgage payments that are more than 35 percent of one's income. A commitment beyond this may well be oppressive and produce anxiety or pressure for the family. Payments much above 35 percent of income must call for other spending adjustments.

VARIETY OF MORTGAGES

Mortgage rates vary according to economic conditions. Thirty-year loans were available at just over 10 percent interest in early 1987. Two years earlier the rates on the same loans exceeded 13 percent. What will be the rate tomorrow? No one knows, of course, but always remember that we have the option of refinancing in the future. Usually refinancing is not viable unless the rate drops about 2 percent below our present rate. Moreover, the closing costs should be redeemed within two years; otherwise, refinancing is questionable except in the case of resale and assumption of an existing mortgage.

Fixed-Rate Mortgage

Fixed-rate mortgages are secured from lending institutions and may be conventional, FHA, or VA (Veterans Administration) loans. Each entails different qualifications and requirements.

The loan is marked by a fixed number of years at a fixed rate and a fixed monthly dollar payment.

The length of loan is generally fifteen, twenty, twenty-five, or thirty years. Of course, the longer the term of the loan, the lower the monthly payment—but the slower the equity gain and the more the total interest paid.

Always be sure that such a loan does not have a prepayment penalty. If it does, an early payoff of the loan will cost something.

Seek a loan that is "assumable," that is, a loan that someone buying your home can take over without the need to negotiate a new loan. This is an advantage when we seek to sell, especially if interest rates have risen considerably since our mortgage was initiated. If the loan is not assumable, our buyer may need to finance at a higher rate, increasing the risk of our making a sale or forcing us to lower our selling price.

Adjustable-Rate Mortgage (ARM)

Adjustable-rate mortgages become popular during periods when interest rates are high and perhaps unstable. The loan usually begins at a lower rate, with the rate gradually increasing either annually or every few years.

ARMs are always linked to a financial index. Make sure you fully understand the government index used and ask for a chart of that index over the last ten years or so. This will reveal the degree of fluctuation and allow for better anticipation of rate increases.

For the borrower's protection, there should be a cap on

interest with an ARM. Most ARMs are offered with a cap of 2 to 4 percent above the original rate and a floor of 1 or 2 percent below it. In addition, seek an ARM that contracts not to increase more then 1 percent per year. Remember, on a $75,000 mortgage, a 1 percent increase boosts the payment about $750 per year or $65 per month! Few of us are prepared to handle a sudden increase like that.

ARMs are advisable only when interest rates are especially high. They also are an advantage if we plan to sell the house within five years.

Biweekly Mortgage

A biweekly mortgage is basically a fixed-rate mortgage with the unique feature that there are twenty-six payments per year rather than twelve. The advantage is that the principal is paid off more quickly over thirty years. This is due to the fact that making twenty-six payments is the equivalent of making an extra month's payment over the course of a year.

A problem is that clergy paid monthly will find it much more difficult to budget for this odd increment.

The savings on a twenty-five- or thirty-year loan are significant. The extra month's payment is applied to reducing the principal. Therefore a thirty-year loan is reduced to twenty years, a savings in interest of one-third during the life of the loan. A $100,000 mortgage for thirty years at 10 percent would, on a biweekly plan, reduce interest from $215,000 to $137,000 over the life of the loan, a savings of more than $77,000. It would also increase equity from $3,470 to $9,269 in the first five years. This doubles the amount of equity applicable to an equity loan.

Only a few lending institutions offer a biweekly mortgage plan, but it is worth asking about it.

The same result can be accomplished simply by making an additional payment whenever possible. Be careful, however, if your loan interest rate is 10 percent and you can invest for 12 percent, lest you actually lose two percent by paying early. An investment in a growth-income fund will usually gain in excess of 12 percent. Invest your extra dollars; be slow to pay off low-interest loans early.

And do not spend carelessly the money you save.

Reverse Annuity Mortgage (RAM)

Some older clergy may want to consider a unique form of financing a retirement annuity called a "reverse annuity mortgage." The bank pays you a monthly annuity or payment for your house, and after an agreed-on number of years or when you and your spouse die, the bank "inherits" the house based on the monthly annuity payments you had received. You have the advantage of a stable, regular monthly income. Medicare benefits are not affected, because the Medicare administrators look at this type of "annuity" as debt and not income. Remember, the bank—not your children—gets the house upon death or maturity.

If a clergyman has limited retirement investments and is going to live virtually on social security, then the RAM is an option to consider. It allows the family to occupy the home for retirement years and assures a regular income. The bank or savings institution would appraise the home, offer a contract, and buy your home through this reverse loan.

ADVICE ON LOANS

I follow one basic principle in taking out loans: I borrow as much as I can cover with income, for as long a period as possible, at as low an interest rate as possible. Why?

1. I will probably be repaying with inflationary dollars. My $700 payment today, given an average inflation rate of 3 percent per year, will be the equivalent of a payment of $385 in the fifteenth year based on today's dollars.

2. Using the loan institution's money allows me to invest my own at higher interest and make a gain over the same period of years. For example, if I use $15,000 as a down payment out of $25,000 available, I have $10,000 left to invest for interest and appreciation. If I use the entire

$25,000 for a down payment I will save only the interest, with no opportunity for appreciation or higher earnings.

3. The higher loan means more interest paid and a higher deductible amount from my gross income. This directly affects my tax obligation. Interest paid on loans is deductible for investment property (with certain limiting factors), a second home, or a vacation home as well as our primary residence.

This kind of thinking runs contrary to my parents' "depression" philosophy of taking out a small mortgage and "paying it off as soon as possible." Times have changed since the Great Depression.

If you need the feeling of security with smaller payments or a quicker reduction of debt, use your cash for a down payment and borrow less.

CONCLUSION

Should a pastor own a home, rent, or use a parsonage? If the option is given, my preference is to own—qualified by location, the local economy, the anticipated length of tenure, and the cost of housing in the area.

The following chart, although soon out of date, compares housing costs across the United States. Before making a move, a pastor who owns a home will want to compare his property with the value of housing in the new locale.

Median Sale Price—Single-Family Homes
(November 1986 compared with November 1985)

City	3rd qtr. 1985	3rd qtr. 1986	%
Albany	$61,000	$75,000	+ 23.0
Albuquerque	81,000	85,400	+ 6.6
Akron	55,400	56,900	+ 2.7
Orange County, Calif.	137,800	149,600	+ 8.6
Baltimore	77,400	78,000	+ 0.8
Baton Rouge	75,500	69,600	-7.8

City	3rd qtr. 1985	3rd qtr. 1986	%
Birmingham, Ala.	65,400	69,800	+6.7
Boston	138,800	165,600	+19.3
Buffalo	46,300	52,800	+14.0
Charlotte, N.C.	69,100	75,400	+9.1
Chicago	82,300	86,700	+5.3
Cincinnati	61,800	64,500	+4.4
Cleveland	67,000	69,100	+3.1
Dallas/Ft. Worth	89,800	92,400	+2.9
Denver	85,900	87,500	+1.9
Des Moines	52,900	55,200	+4.3
Detroit	52,600	59,900	+13.9
Grand Rapids	48,300	50,600	+4.8
Hartford	102,000	132,000	+29.4
Houston	83,700	70,400	-15.9
Indianapolis	55,300	59,900	+8.3
Kansas City, Mo.	61,000	64,000	+4.9
Louisville	51,400	53,700	+4.5
Memphis	67,200	71,500	+6.4
Milwaukee	66,700	70,800	+6.1
Minneapolis/St. Paul	75,900	78,100	+2.9
New York	135,200	166,800	+20.7
Omaha	59,800	58,500	-2.2
Orlando	72,400	73,600	+1.7
Philadelphia	71,700	75,600	+5.4
Phoenix	73,400	79,100	+7.8
Portland, Ore.	63,200	63,100	-0.2
Providence	69,800	91,900	+31.7
St. Louis	68,800	72,000	+4.7
San Diego	109,300	121,100	+10.8
San Francisco	143,600	164,900	+14.7
Tampa	60,300	64,300	+6.6
Tulsa	66,300	65,600	-1.1
Washington, D.C.	98,300	98,900	+0.6
USA Total/Avg.	76,600	80,200	+4.7

(Source: National Association of Realtors)

9 | SAVINGS AND INVESTMENT INSTRUMENTS

What happens if there are a few dollars left over in the bank account at the end of the month? Is this available for savings accounts or growth investments? Extra dollars should be considered for investment.

There is a wide range of investment instruments and options. Salesmen, brokers, and a whole host of advisers are ready to help us "make money." Before we release those hard-earned and not easily saved dollars, we should take the time to understand the variety of investment instruments available.

TYPES OF INSTRUMENTS

Insured Bank and Thrift Accounts

Insured savings accounts are solid and safe up to $100,000, but they hardly build a financial future. Today these accounts return just over 5 percent.

NOW and Passbook Accounts

NOW and passbook accounts will range from a combination checking/savings account commonly termed a NOW (negotiable order of withdrawal) account to the common passbook savings account.

The wise investor will use a NOW checking account that requires a minimum balance (with a range of $300 to $1,500). This way the checkbook account does not simply "sit" without interest. Be aware, most of these accounts will penalize with a service charge if the balance falls below the agreed minimum balance. It may be profitable to shop around at a number of banks or savings and loans for this account, because terms vary from place to place. NOW accounts will generally pay at the same rate as a regular passbook savings account.

I have banked for nearly twenty years at a bank that is about 100 miles from my home. The rates are excellent, and the terms on NOW accounts better than most. I do my banking by mail; there is no need to appear in person.

A passbook savings account is basic to all savings. My first experience with the world of finance came with passbook savings, and as a teenager I remember the monthly entries in that special 2½-by-4-inch book. The problem with the passbook is that the interest rate is low compared with other kinds of savings accounts; even though the security and liquidity aspects rate high, the earnings are poor. Anyone with a NOW checking account does not need a passbook savings account.

The NOW and passbook accounts are actually ready money "parking places." Everyone should have at least three months' expenses covered in such accounts in case of emergency, but to keep more than that amount is counter-productive.

Certificates of Deposit (CDs)

Certificates of deposit are savings accounts that promise a fixed rate over a fixed amount of time, usually from three months up to ten years. These rates are keyed to the federal Treasury bill rates for a prescribed amount of time. The longer the term of investment, the higher the rate offered.

The fixed rate of return allows us to project exactly what the investment will earn. Another advantage is that CDs are fully insured up to $100,000 by the federal government in banks or savings and loan institutions.

These deposit accounts will fluctuate by 1½ percent according to the geographic area. Be aware that not all financial institutions are insured by the federal government through FDIC (Federal Deposit Insurance Corporation) or FSLIC (Federal Savings and Loan Insurance Corporation). Whether you hold your CDs in your own city or county or at a distance, check on the stability of the institution with which you invest. You may also check whether an institution is on the government "watch list"—available from the FDIC or the FSLIC.

I suggest that CDs make a good investment when interest rates are high (13 to 14 percent in 1981–82) and assign the maximum period of time. A problem arises when high-interest CDs come due in low-interest times. Today investors are finding that the 13–14 percent CDs that come to maturity now will draw no more than 7 percent return, a drop of 50 percent in earnings. This kind of loss could devastate the financial plans of retired clergy.

A warning must be given regarding the early call of CDs. If we desire to claim our money before the deposit note's due date, we will pay handsomely, because a penalty charge is assessed that can negate some of our earnings.

U.S. Savings Bonds

Savings bonds rates were reduced in fall 1986 to 6 percent interest. U.S. savings bonds are now marginal as an investment tool, yet they remain one of the easiest ways to save with small amounts.

There are some advantages to savings bonds. First, the interest accrued is deferred for tax purposes until the bonds come due. Second, the bonds can be purchased in low denominations and without a fee or commission. Savings bonds begin at $25 face value. Of course, these bonds are also fully insured by the federal government.

In fact, all the accounts described to this point have the security of federal insurance up to $100,000. Each spouse can have an account, and there can be a joint account. So we actually can be secure for up to $300,000 in federally insured institutions.

Other investment instruments will not offer the insured safety of these plans, but with risk the interest, growth, and appreciation all increase.

Money Market Mutual Funds

Money market mutual funds are not limited to "mutual" companies but are also offered through the conventional savings and loan institutions and banks.

The money in these accounts is invested in "short-term paper," Treasury bills, the safest of jumbo CDs, repurchase agreements, and commercial paper (short-term borrowings of major consumer companies such as Sears Roebuck, General Motors, or General Electric).

The safety record is impeccable. The money is very fluid. I believe that this type of account, probably in a mutual fund where transfer privileges are available, should be a part of everyone's investment package. If placed in a "family" of mutual funds, it provides the freedom to switch from one fund to another with a small charge.

These money markets may be entered with low minimums, and they provide yields that outperform short-term CDs most of the time and passbook accounts all the time. A money market account becomes a building block for a financial future, and it also offers a place to "park" money that is in transition from stocks and bonds. A minimum balance of $500 to $1,000 is generally required to open or to maintain the account.

Some excellent features may be available with these accounts, including check writing, comparably high interest, and the flexibility of transfer to other accounts within the same family of funds. The financial pages of major newspapers will usually report the rates.

Single Premium Deferred Annuity

A single premium deferred annuity basically combines an annuity with life insurance. This is a very conservative investment tool and is best for clergy who have a high tax liability or are willing to tolerate an inflexible program. It may not be the wisest investment in inflationary times, since the annuity interest paid is generally conservative. This insurance annuity and single-payment life insurance package, however, has become a popular investment tool.

MUTUAL FUNDS

Mutual funds are a phenomenon in the investment world. The dollars invested have now surpassed those in banks and savings and loan institutions. A few funds are approaching the billion-dollar figure in deposits. There are many kinds of funds in scores of fund families.

What is a mutual fund? It is a grouping of small investors' money for the purpose of purchasing stocks and bonds for growth and income. Mutual funds vary in character and purpose. We must receive and read a "prospectus" before purchasing a fund. This will state the purpose of the fund, its assets, the percent invested in each industry, and a list of holdings over the last three months. The prospectus should also share an annualized yield for comparison and give information of changes to the account. Always check the performance of the fund over the past ten years.

Several guides to mutual fund companies are available. Among them are the "Guide to Mutual Funds" published by the Investment Company Institute, 1600 M Street NW, Washington, DC 20036; and a directory to no-load funds published by the No-Load Mutual Fund Association, P.O. Box 2004, JAF Building, New York, NY 10116.

Even clergy with a denominational pension plan should consider a 403(B) plan for mutual fund investment.

Income Funds

Income funds have income as their goal rather than appreciation or growth. Funds of this nature will be invested in bonds, CDs, and "blue chip" (high-dividend) stocks. Income funds can be "sectored" in a family of funds, and this can cater to either conservative or aggressive tastes. If income with safety is our purpose, we will find a suitable fund; if we seek a high-income fund entailing greater risks, we can find that, too. There is something for everyone.

Growth/Income Funds

Growth/income funds seek to balance income with stock value appreciation. The goal is to select stocks from the three major U.S. exchanges, often paying some dividends but with capital appreciation as a primary goal. Have these been successful? Yes, on the whole this group of funds has outperformed all other categories over a ten-year period.

Most clergy should consider this kind of fund in their investment portfolio. The risks are minimal except in a recession period, and the advantage is some accrued income plus appreciation. This allows for a measure of safety with some growth. I have had one of these funds for about ten years, and it has appreciated more than 260 percent in value. These are not funds that one jumps into and out of amid fluctuations in the stock market.

Clergy under fifty-five years of age should choose a fund, add to it on a regular schedule, and let it increase over the years. Survey its history every five years along with a check of your financial plan and then decide whether to retain or sell this fund. If you have chosen a fund from this group for a 403(B) investment, I would stick with it, especially if you have chosen a fund with a good ten-year record and you are under fifty-five.

This type of fund should be the foundation of our financial plan until we reach retirement. Such a fund will usually mirror the vicissitudes of the American economy and should protect our investments from inflation.

Aggressive Growth Funds

Aggressive growth funds are a different matter. The purpose is growth or appreciation. Producing income has a low priority. These funds will buy in all three exchanges and also purchase stock from new offerings of smaller companies; venture companies with potential may be included in the portfolio of this type of fund.

Funds with an aggressive purpose have had a mixed history over the past ten years. Some have led the entire mutual fund market, while others have lagged behind growth/income funds.

It is more difficult to select a "winner" in this area, but as with all funds, we are "buying" the manager's expertise and record. Again, check the record over five and ten years.

Younger clergy would possibly consider up to 25 percent of their retirement dollars in such a fund. An aggressive growth fund is much more speculative and will have wide fluctuations on daily performance. Due to their speculative and aggressive nature, these funds must be watched carefully. Again, if we choose a fund with a good record, our concerns will be eased. The aggressive funds require patience and a long view.

Sector Funds

Sector, or select, funds are the newest phenomenon in the mutual fund market. Basically, instead of buying stock across all the markets, these funds home in on one sector— that is, select one industry in the economy. This gives the investor the option to invest in a specific field such as aerospace, chemicals, computers, health care, overseas corporations, or utilities. The list goes on. One family of funds, Fidelity Investments in Boston, offers more than thirty select or sector funds.

The advantage of this kind of fund is that we are able to choose a certain industry. The risk is that a downturn in the industry may leave us in jeopardy. This is a choice only for the knowledgeable and venturesome. I do not recommend that a novice participate. An investor must be aware of industry trends and respond to a switch of funds on short notice. It is less risky than buying one or two stocks in the market, but still means much more involvement than any of the other groups. If you are familiar with a particular sector of industry, this kind of fund might have interest for you.

There is a moral aspect to sector funds of which clergy should take note. Most growth and income funds will, from time to time, invest in the tobacco and liquor industries. We can avoid investing in these kinds of stocks through a sector fund that is compatible with our personal beliefs.

All growth, growth/income, and sector funds should be evaluated in comparison with the year to date average of the Standard and Poors 500 (that is, 500 representative stocks). If the fund does not keep up with the S&P 500, we should carefully evaluate our choice, because we are below the average market growth. It is best to do this evaluation before investment by surveying a fund's history. Be aware that a fund may not match the S&P 500 average in every year.

Tax-free Funds

Few clergy will ever need to consider tax-free funds, but they are available, even sectored, in certain states such as California, New York, Massachusetts, and Minnesota.

These funds invest in municipal bonds, whose earnings are tax free. Such a fund has value only for clergy in a high tax bracket. The income return presently ranges between 5 and 8½ percent, and for a person in a high tax bracket this would amount to 28 to 37 percent in real dollars, since this would be your tax percentage on earnings. The Tax Reform Act of 1986 will probably have an impact on this type of fund.

Family Funds

The term "family funds" needs some explanation. Mutual funds are usually grouped under one company. Some of the leaders in the field are Fidelity, Value Line, Vanguard, and Templeton. These are "families," and each will have "children," or different funds from income to sector within the "family." I believe it is wise to buy a mutual fund within a large family—in other words, a fund with numerous options. Switching funds then becomes a simple procedure. Most "family funds" allow switching by phone.

Load/Low-load/No-load Funds

Mutual funds are in the business to make money, not only for us, but for the company. Therefore, funds are purchased with one of three "charges," or designations, concerning cost: load, low-load, or no-load.

Load. The load is a percentage of commission charged for purchase. This amount may be as high as 8½ percent on each transaction. Therefore our return may in fact become a deficit, depending on the "load" that it must make up in earnings. A fund needs to outperform a "load." If the success of a load fund is such that it is achieving earnings above low- or no-load funds, perhaps they merit purchase. Generally I would discourage purchase of any "load" fund.

Low-load. Some funds have initiated a charge of up to 3 percent, due to the success they have achieved or due to the cost of doing business. Fidelity's Magellan fund for years was a "no-load" fund and recently initiated a 3 percent charge. The point to remember is that for the past ten years Magellan has had a phenomenal return. A 3 percent charge is probably merited with exceptional results. There is no disadvantage in paying a low-load commission when a fund has an excellent record.

No-load. Some people will dispute the term "no-load" because every fund charges for its service. It is true that no-load funds will charge off expenses that probably amount to 1 to 2 percent before making distributions; but there are no commission charges assessed to "no-loads." I prefer to invest in a no-load fund, for it puts all my dollars to work. The record for no-loads has been equal to or has exceeded the average for "load" funds. Appendix B will reveal how to keep track of your mutual fund worth.

Read the prospectus carefully. It is your money, and you should know as much about its "home" as possible.

GUIDELINES FOR MUTUAL FUND INVESTMENT

1. *Get started!* Some funds require as little as $100 to open an account and may be added to in increments of $25 or more.

2. *Find the dollar-cost average.* This term will be dealt with more fully in another chapter. It is simply investing monthly or quarterly rather then once a year, and it means we will not need to be caught at a "high price" time. The cost will average itself out over a year's time and avert the consequences of fluctuations between highs and lows.

3. *Research a fund's history.* A public library will have information concerning most funds. *Money* magazine pub-

lishes the results of some funds monthly. Both *Money* and *Forbes* publish an annual performance list of funds. A variety of services is available for evaluating fund performances.

4. *Buy history*. New funds have not had experience, so should we risk investing in a new fund when excellent funds with good earnings records are available? A new fund needs time to develop, so I recommend that you not risk your money on one when mature funds are available.

5. *Buy no-load or low-load funds*. Investing in one of these funds obviously means more of our money gets invested. There is usually no reason to buy a mutual fund through brokers. We can be sure a fee will be charged by a broker. Buy directly from the company whenever possible. Funds purchased through a broker will seldom be a bargain.

6. *Buy a good fund—and forget it!* Income and growth funds especially should not need a great measure of care. A review of our financial plan every five years is generally enough care until we reach fifty-five years of age.

7. *Reinvest earnings*. Until retirement, all earnings should be reinvested. This means we will be purchasing additional shares. Remember, if we take the earnings, we must pay taxes. Capital gains are taxable each year, but regular earnings should be reinvested and thereby compounded.

8. *Use all the services of the fund family:* Each fund family will have different requirements and services. Choose a fund family that offers "phone switching." This allows us, using a preassigned code or number, to switch from fund to fund. Most funds will levy a small charge for any transfer.

Some funds offer a detailed report only quarterly or annually. I prefer a fund family that gives a monthly update of the account.

EVALUATING FUND FAMILIES

It is not appropriate for me to make specific recommendations regarding investments. However, I shall mention four fund families (not individual funds) that I have invested in or have watched carefully over a number of years: Fidelity Management, Kemper Financial Services, Dreyfus Corporation, and the Vanguard Group.

Hundreds of other funds are available. Do your own research, but follow the guidelines. As mentioned earlier, *Forbes* magazine publishes a performance review of funds in a late August/early September issue each year, and *Money* magazine does the same once a year. *Consumer Reports* magazine offered an extensive evaluation for the first time in its June 1987 issue.

10 | INVESTMENTS FOR EACH FINANCIAL AGE

All clergy should begin to make investments at some point in their lives. Denominational plans will be the first choice of investment for many, especially if the church offers a program of matching funds.

A denominational plan will usually allow at least two options: an annuity type of investment that will assure a certain amount of return at retirement; or a mutual variable fund type of account that will fluctuate with the market. If these alternatives are offered and you are allowed to divide your resources between them, a basic rule to follow is this:

Under 40 years old	25% in annuity
	75% in variable fund
40–55 years old	50% in annuity
	50% in variable fund
55–Retirement	75–100% in annuity
	Invest in variable fund only during strong or inflationary economy

This is admittedly a conservative plan, and clergy not planning to retire until age seventy may consider putting 25 percent into the variable fund until at least age sixty-two.

Denominational plans are usually low-risk and conservative. If more investment money is available, it is wise to place it in a growth/income or aggressive growth fund.

A problem with some denominational plans is the

matter of "vesting," which is the right for an investor to withdraw money on demand. This right is often restricted until a person has been in a plan for a certain number of years or reaches a certain age. A retirement account should be vested to serve its purpose best, and ages 59, 62, and 65 are common options. The philosophy behind nonvesting is to preserve the funds intact until they are needed at retirement.

Clergy are eligible for a 403(B) even though they are participating in a denominational or institutional plan. A 403(B), referred to earlier, is a deferred-income pension plan applicable only to employees of nonprofit organizations or educational institutions. A percentage of salary is set aside, with taxes deferred until it is distributed, usually at retirement when tax consequences are less. Both the church and the employee may contribute, but all funds are deposited by the church. All the funds are tax deferred and are fully vested, that is, under the control of the employee.

The 403(B) must be set up by the church or institution. The plan is easily set up by the church treasurer's working with a major mutual fund company. Since money invested in a 403(B) is tax deferred, it should not be reported on a gross earnings report, a 1099, or a W2 form.

Clergy without a denominational retirement plan should turn to a 403(B) account. Note that beginning in 1989 there will be tax of 10 percent on funds withdrawn from a 403(B). Another option is an IRA if you meet the criteria. The IRA has lost some of its availability and appeal under the new tax law.

Let us consider the case of a clergyman with a 403(B). I suggest an investment policy according to age as follows:

Age 40 or under

60%	Aggressive growth fund
30%	Growth/income fund
5%	Precious metals/gold fund
5%	High-income fund

Ages 40 to 55

50%	Growth/income fund

30%   Aggressive growth fund
10%   High-income fund
10%   Government securities/cash reserve fund

Age 55 to retirement (or up to five years before retirement)

50%   Growth/income fund
30%   Government securities/cash reserve fund
10%   Aggressive growth fund
10%   Precious metals/gold fund

These are merely guidelines. Preference should be given to investing within one family of funds so that transfer is simple and inexpensive. Remember to evaluate the portfolio every five years until age fifty-five, then do it annually.

Aggressive growth funds are designed to add capital appreciation to the investment savings. They entail additional risk, of course, but this is where the "nest egg" is built in early years.

Growth/income funds are designed to invest in major, well-known companies. These funds will seek some appreciation, but mainly with stock that pays dividends. The risk is lower than in the aggressive funds.

GOVERNMENT SECURITIES/
MONEY MARKETS

The government securities and money markets form a hedge against bad times and are often used to "park" money while considering a change in investment options. Such funds are safe, but the return on investment is relatively low except in inflationary times.

PRECIOUS METALS/GOLD FUNDS

Most financial advisers would expect some investment to be made in gold or other precious metals. The easiest and cheapest way is through a mutual fund that purchases bullion or invests in precious metal mining companies. The value of such an account is used as a hedge against inflationary periods. Gold prices usually rise dramatically during those times.

How should you invest: Once a year? Quarterly? Monthly? The answer lies in dollar-cost averaging. This works best with monthly contributions.

DOLLAR-COST AVERAGING

The dollar-cost averaging plan is one of the best ways for small investors such as clergy to cover the stock market's ups and downs. It consists basically of buying into funds on the installment plan; you invest a fixed amount of money at regular intervals, regardless of what is happening monthly on the stock market.

The strategy is simply this: Dollars buy less stock in the fund when the market is high, more stock when the market is low. If we have made quarterly or monthly payments, we have not put ourselves at risk by buying a large quantity at the highest time period of the year; rather, the purchases made at regular intervals will generally average out through high and low times to our advantage. The downside risk is greatly alleviated with dollar-cost averaging.

Mutual funds continue to be the best place to do dollar-cost averaging, since they are broad based and fall or rise with the market conditions. They also allow you to invest in small amounts monthly or quarterly. Church treasurers generally prefer to write one check a year for this benefit, but urge them to send checks monthly or at least quarterly.

What about clergy who cannot afford more than a few dollars in investment? The most important aspect of investing is getting started. Then keep it going, whether through dimes in a jar or hundreds of dollars per month.

Let's get started. How about twenty-five dollars per month? Purchase a twenty-five-dollar U.S. Savings Bond once a month, or put the same amount in a no-load, low-entry mutual fund. Now you are on your way. Years from now you will be surprised how this investment has grown.

11 | *THE COST OF COLLEGE*

The responsibility of financing a college education for children can be awesome and frightening for clergy families. A family with three children will discover that the cost of education, including financial aid from outside sources, will be greater than the cost of any home the family may own.

The costs at a private Christian college averaged $10,000 a year in 1986, including tuition, room and board, books, and incidental expenses. Some major institutions, such as Ivy League colleges, cost up to $20,000 per year.

Higher education for our children is helped in many instances by community colleges and state universities, which cost considerably less than private institutions. But for those who desire a denominational college or another Christian college (often a parent's alma mater), clergy income often falls above the federal grant income level but too low to finance education from family resources. This problem, in fact, is typical of many middle-class families in the United States, not just clergy.

THE FINANCIAL AID FORM

All colleges offer some kind of tuition aid or a tuition loan plan. Financial aid begins with the parents completing a Financial Aid Form (FAF). This application form, administered by the College Scholarship Service (CSS), is available from all colleges and from most high school counseling offices. There is a small fee for this service. If we are applying only for federal aid, we may use the free "Application for Federal Aid." It is available wherever FAFs are offered.

The FAF is necessary if we are applying for (1) financial aid from a college, (2) a state scholarship or grant, or (3) a federal grant program such as a Pell Grant. All questions must be answered carefully on the FAF. It currently includes 59 questions, some with several parts.

The FAF should not be sent until the beginning of the year in which the person is planning to enter college. The form should be completed as soon as the parents' tax return is completed, since some income information is required. Forms for first-time students must normally be filed earlier than those for returning students, but all should be filed before May 1. Check with the college financial aid office for the recommended date.

Some colleges may request a copy of your tax return for verifying information. This should always be sent to the college, not to the College Scholarship Service.

The CSS will send an acknowledgment to the parents and an evaluation to the college or colleges indicated on the FAF. We may choose to have the evaluation sent to as many as eight different schools, but for each one a small amount is added to the FAF fee.

Cost – Resources = Need is the formula for financial aid. The factors normally included are tuition, fees, estimated cost of books and supplies, room and board, transportation, and personal expenses.

Resources of the family are always weighed by such things as financial obligations and the number of dependents. Relevant factors for evaluating the expected family contribution include parental income and assets, any outside assistance such as social security or veteran's benefits, scholarships, the student's assets, and expected savings from summer employment. There may be other factors besides financial condition. For example, a minimum grade point average or a minimum score on the standard high school examinations (SAT or ACT) may be required.

Usually financial aid recipients must be enrolled at least half-time and must make satisfactory academic progress.

Here are some reminders regarding the FAF:

1. Apply as soon as possible, because every school has limited funds available.

2. Be ready, if needed, to share IRS tax returns with the desired college.

3. Complete the forms carefully, leaving nothing blank.

4. Mail the FAF on time, and enclose the necessary fees.

5. Include your social security number on the FAF.

WORK-STUDY EMPLOYMENT

Another opportunity for financial aid is Work-Study Employment. This is designed for needy students who may earn a portion of their expenses through part-time work on campus jobs. These jobs are limited to students who have completed financial aid applications and demonstrate need. The jobs will range from custodial assistants to library aides. Colleges do not guarantee placement.

A student approved for work-study employment is allocated a specific number of hours based on his or her financial need, ranging from eight to fifteen hours per week. Earnings will range from $800 to $1,500 for the full school year's employment, depending on the hourly rate. The wages are always paid directly to the student. Earnings are to be used for educational purposes and should be applied by the student to the account balance at the college.

The student's employer must be satisfied with the work performance for the job to continue.

GRANTS, SCHOLARSHIPS, AND LOANS

A number of grants, scholarships, and loans are available based on a student's need. Grants and scholarships, unlike loans, do not need to be repaid.

Pell Basic Grant

The Pell Basic Grant is a federally funded program that may cover up to 60 percent of the cost of education based on some strict criteria. The need analysis includes the cost of child care or disability care.

The maximum amount of a grant reached $2,300 per person in 1987 and was scheduled to rise to $2,500 in 1988; $2,700 in 1989; $2,900 in 1990; and $3,100 in 1991.

Supplemental Educational Opportunity Grants

The Supplemental Educational Opportunity Grant (SEOG) is a grant for students with exceptional need. The funds are provided by the federal government and administered by colleges. The maximum amount is now $4,000, and the minimum amount has been reduced to $100. This grant may be received in addition to the Pell Grant.

State Scholarship Grants

Some states have excellent grant programs. Illinois now provides more than $3,000 per year for students with need. Michigan provides grants to residents attending private colleges within the state to offset some of the cost differences between public and private institutions.

Each state has certain criteria for its grants. Usually the grant is given only for a student attending a college within the state. Some states have reciprocal grant agreements with other states that allow for greater choice of where to attend college without losing financial aid eligibility. Check on the particular program offered in your state.

Perkins Loan

The Carl Perkins Loan Fund, formerly known as the National Direct Student Loan, is a federal program based on a student's financial need. It is administered by colleges. The loan limits are now $4,500 for freshman and sophomores, $9,000 for juniors and seniors, and $18,000 for graduate and professional students.

Loan repayment must begin nine months after leaving school or at any time a student drops below half-time status.

Loan cancellations are made for Peace Corps or VISTA service and for teaching Head Start or special education or teaching in designated schools serving low-income students.

The interest on Perkins Loans carries an interest rate of 5 percent, which is lower than conventional finance charges.

Guaranteed Student Loan

The Guaranteed Student Loan program requires an application form separate from the FAF. The application is available at any bank that participates in this program. This program differs in part from the Perkins Loan in that the funds are borrowed from banking institutions rather than the federal government, which merely insures the loans.

Annual loan limits have risen to $2,625 for freshman and sophomores, $4,000 for juniors and seniors, and $7,500 for graduate students. The aggregate limit for underclassmen is $17,250; $54,750 is the cumulative total allowed for combined undergraduate and postgraduate study.

For loans made after July 1, 1988, the 8 percent interest rate will remain for the first four years of repayment, rising to 10 percent in the fifth year. Borrowers must pay a 3 percent insurance premium, but the amount may be included in the loan.

Repayment begins six months after graduation or at any time that the student drops below half-time status.

Parent Loans for Undergraduate Students

The program known as Parent Loans for Undergraduate Students (PLUS) is less attractive than other loans because of the high interest rate of 12 percent. But these rates are in line with other personal loan rates from commercial institutions, which range from 2 to 4 percent higher than loans from federal programs.

The loan application is available at cooperating banks. The loan limit is $4,000 per year, with a cumulative $20,000 total. The interest rate is variable at 3.75 percent above the Treasury bill (T-bill) rate, with a 12 percent cap.

This program is an option for parents who choose to finance a part of the education with a personal loan. It is an alternative to a home-equity loan or a personal commercial loan. It is based on credit standing, not student need. Repayment begins sixty days after the funds are disbursed.

College-funded Scholarships and Grants

Every college has certain scholarship funds available in the general operations budget. These will have special criteria, but all are grants. They may have such names as Presidential Scholarship, Dean's Scholarship, special ability grants (designated for special fields such as athletics, music, or writing), denominational grants, or clergy discounts.

Many of these will be limited to students who have attained a certain grade point average or ACT/SAT scores. The college catalog and financial aid officer are the best sources of information on scholarships and grants.

OTHER WAYS TO FINANCE AN EDUCATION

There are several ways to pay for an education that are not considered student financial aid.

Commercial Loans

For families who do not qualify for financial aid, there are various programs at commercial institutions that can be used for educational loans. Every college financial aid office will have a list of companies that it recommends for an installment loan program.

Knight Insurance Extended Repayment

The rate of interest under the Knight Insurance Extended Repayment plan is presently just over 10 percent with a ten-year term. The loan will be given to cover 100 percent of college costs, and there are no educational restrictions to people who have the credit standing to qualify.

Mellon Bank Edu-check

For the Mellon Bank Edu-check, the rate of interest is presently above 12 percent with an eight-year term. The loan will cover 100 percent of college costs.

Tuition Plan

The rate of interest varies for Tuition Plan loans. The term is ten years and covers 100 percent of college costs. The borrower must be a resident of one of the thirty-eight participating states.

Home Equity Loans

The Tax Reform Law of 1986 provides that the interest on a home equity loan used for education is deductible (because it is a home equity loan), even though the interest on student loans is not (because they are regarded as consumer loans). Thus it offers a small tax break. Usually the interest charge will be less than commercial loans, but probably more than government-secured loans such as the Perkins or Guaranteed Student Loan programs.

FINANCIAL AWARD LETTER

Nearly 70 percent of all college students receive some form of financial aid. At some time after the FAF has been evaluated, the applicant has been accepted by a college, and the tuition deposit fee (typically $100) has been paid, the student will receive a "Financial Aid Award Letter" from the college. This will list all grants and loans for which the student is eligible, Work-Study Employment eligibility, and the expected family contribution.

The family share can sometimes be decreased by a variety of the loan plans spelled out in the award letter.

The award letter is in essence a contract covering the financial conditions for a year of study.

ESTABLISHING INDEPENDENCE FOR NEED

Until 1987, students could declare their independence if they were not claimed on their parents' tax return for two years, did not live with their parents more than six weeks during either year, and did not receive more that $750 parental support during either year. This enabled some students access to grants and loans that were not available to them as dependents due to the family's level of income.

Now the criteria have been changed. An independent student is now defined as one who is age twenty-four or older, is an orphan or a ward of the court, and has documented self-sufficiency by earning at least $4,000 a year, or is a veteran. These changes greatly curtail eligibility for independent status.

GRADE MINIMUMS

Students receiving federal aid must now maintain a "C" average by the end of their second year in college or have a standing that is consistent with graduation requirements. This new regulation serves to reward the serious student.

ENDOWED TUITION PLANS

A new method of tuition payment has recently been initiated by a number of colleges. Parents or grandparents can now begin to pay in advance for a student's college education. The younger the child when the program begins, the greater the benefits later on.

For example, suppose your child will be eligible for college in the year 2000. The college estimates what the cost of a year's education will be in that year and how much it can earn by investing your money now. If college costs increase an average of 7½ percent per year until A.D. 2000, then what costs $10,000 in 1987 could come to $20,000 then. The college may ask for an endowment of $6,000 for one-year's tuition and invest the money, hoping that it will double every seven years. The college will gain a few thousand dollars from the investment and has already enrolled one student for the year 2000.

This plan has some drawbacks, primarily that the student is forced to attend a particular college, at least at first, without a choice. Therefore, parents and grandparents might want to limit their investment to only one year at their favored denominational college or alma mater and give the student a choice for succeeding years.

APPLYING FOR FINANCIAL AID

Consider these suggestions in seeking financial aid:

1. Complete the Financial Aid Form (FAF) as described earlier in the chapter.

2. Seek grants and scholarships from Christian colleges, especially since there are usually a number of them earmarked for clergy families.

3. Apply for academic scholarships from foundations, corporations, and government agencies.

4. Feel free to call the college financial aid office for help.

5. You may want to purchase the following publications from Octameron Associates, Alexandria, Virginia:

Robert and Anna Reider, *Don't Miss Out: The Ambitious Student's Guide to Financial Aid.*

Victoria A. Fabisch, *The A's + B's: Your Guide to Academic Scholarships.*

The means to pay the huge, looming cost of college are attainable. The family must work together; the result will be a fine education.

12 | SOCIAL SECURITY: INVESTMENT OR INSURANCE?

Just a generation ago social security benefits were the hope of retirement income for clergy beginning their ministerial careers. From the late 1930s, financial security could be secured through the eventual hope of social security payments at retirement. The economy and inflation problems of the 1970s led to concern for the future of the social security program in the early 1980s.

In the late seventies Congress initiated reforms that encouraged private savings. The results were programs such as IRAs, 403(B) plans, and liberalized tax shelters. The eighties produced low inflation and a restructuring of social security funding. Then came the Tax Reform Act of 1986 that eliminated IRAs as tax shelters for most of us and lowered the personal contribution to 403(B) plans. In my opinion this was a backward step for financial security.

The question remains, will social security be solvent in our retirement days? I believe that social security is a political sacred cow and therefore will be ensured solvency, but only with adjustments in both payout terms and a constantly increasing maximum income amount on which the tax is based. Thus our children increasingly will pay for our benefits.

It has been stated that more than 50 percent of the taxpayers contribute more in social security taxes than in federal income taxes. The percentage is probably even higher among clergy.

Clergy are considered by the IRS to be self-employed. We must pay social security contributions on income earned as a minister. Self-employed social security taxes are considerably higher than those paid by someone who is another person's employee, because the employer himself contributes an equal share of the social security tax.

EXEMPTION FROM SOCIAL SECURITY

The option not to join the social security program is available in the first two years of ordination or licensing. This option applies only to income earned as a minister.

The exemption must be applied for on IRS Form 4361. The reason for exemption cannot be economic. The rule is clear that the exemption must be on the grounds that one is conscientiously opposed to accepting benefits from public sources based on religious principles and convictions. The best proof is for the person seeking exemption to have established a private retirement account in lieu of a government plan. Such a plan should be started prior to filing the waiver request.

If you have held credentials longer than two years, you *must* contribute to social security; you no longer have a choice. For additional information, request the social security publications from your local IRS office.

PAYING SOCIAL SECURITY

A social security payment should be made quarterly along with your estimated income tax. These payments are due by 15 April, 15 June, 15 September, and 15 January.

Most tax advisers recommend that clergy include their housing allowance in the social security income base. Some suggest, however, that parsonages, or manses, should not be included in determining the social security gross income, because where there is a parsonage, the option of a housing purchase usually has not been offered.

There are some basic procedures to be followed in handling social security matters. First, whenever there is a name change, the social security office should be informed. Second, check that the social security department has your correct address and social security number. Third, request a written statement from the Social Security Administration every three to five years.

A social security office can supply a "Request for Statement of Earnings." After receiving the response, compare it with your past income tax returns. If there is a discrepancy, follow the proscribed instructions for recovery.

Generally, ten years or forty "quarters" of work during that time must be validated in order to collect benefits. If we will reach age sixty-two by 1991, the ten-year/forty-quarter rule applies. If we reach sixty-two before 1991, the amount of time is reduced by one quarter per year to a floor of eight and one-half years for those retiring in 1985. If we are older than fifty-five and work for a church or nonprofit organization, we can qualify for benefits if we can work up to five more years—the actual number being dependent on our age on 1 January 1984.

RECEIVING BENEFITS

The social security law was amended in 1983, raising the retirement age limit for receiving full benefits. The following table indicates how this age escalation affects us:

Year of Birth	Year Reach 62	Full Benefit Age
1937 or under	1999 or earlier	65
1938	2000	65, 2mo.
1939	2001	65, 4mo.
1940	2002	65, 6mo.
1941	2003	65, 8mo.
1942	2004	65, 10mo.
1943–1954	2005–2016	66
1955	2017	66, 2mo.
1956	2018	66, 4mo.
1957	2019	66, 6mo.
1958	2020	66, 8mo.
1959	2021	66, 10mo.
1960–later	2022–	67

Some clergy may want to retire earlier than sixty-five years of age, or the required age by birth. Early retirement benefits will be reduced by five-ninths of 1 percent for every month prior to sixty-five or the date when the full benefit is due. The formulas apply to spouse, widow, or widower.

Later retirement can increase the social security annual benefit. Those born between 1917 and 1924 will receive 0.25 percent increase or up to 3 percent per year in benefits. Those born in 1925 or later will be increased 0.5 percent every year up to 8 percent for those born in 1943.

The risk is actuarial: less money over a longer period of time, or more money over a shorter period.

Add to this another factor. A person can earn (in 1986) $7,800 per year that is exempt from taxation. (A person retiring before sixty-five has exempt earnings of $5,760.) The amount is raised annually based on cost-of-living adjustments. If earnings surpass these amounts, the benefits will be reduced $1 for every $2 earned over the minimum. Beginning in 1990, the penalty will be eased to $1 cut from benefits for every $3 earned. At seventy years of age the restriction on earnings is removed.

Clergy should not forget that a housing allowance and certain expenses may carry over into retirement years. This certainly will affect one's tax liability in retirement.

Social security payments are also affected by annual COLAs (cost-of-living adjustments). If the cost of living, measured by the Consumer Price Index (CPI), is 3 percent or more, the adjustment is made automatically in the January check. If the CPI is under 3 percent, there is normally no adjustment. (The Congress deviated from this rule in a recent year and provided an adjustment even though the CPI was under 3 percent.)

The benefits for those in the social security program are available at times other than retirement. Our payments obtain a significant disability plan and death annuity if we die before our children reach eighteen years of age.

The disability benefit allows for prorated benefits up to

the time of normal retirement. It is best augmented by a good disability insurance policy.

The death benefit provides for a monthly stipend for each child under eighteen years of age and continues until his or her nineteenth birthday.

It has been estimated that for a person thirty-five years of age with three children, the survivors' benefit could amount to nearly $500,000. The disability insurance at the same age would probably accumulate to $300,000.

This does not mean that social security is a great financial plan for the payer. On the contrary, most of us would have potentially higher benefits if we funded our own programs. Yet the social security program does have some advantages.

How do we initiate benefits? The Social Security Administration will not automatically send us a check. We must file prior to our sixty-fifth birthday at the nearest social security office. The office will inform us as to the records we should provide. Remember, Medicare coverage also must be applied for, and it must take effect before the date we begin receiving our retirement payments, if that date is after our sixty-fifth birthday.

A direct deposit of our check can be made to a bank, a savings and loan institution, or a mutual fund. The financial institution will help you with the procedure.

It is important that clergy do not plan on social security benefits for major retirement needs. Most of us will need significant retirement funds in addition to social security to survive retirement years with financial safety.

13 | RETIREMENT: PLANNING FOR TOMORROW

When does retirement planning begin? It is not frivolous to say that retirement planning begins with the first salary check in the first pastorate. It is difficult for twenty-five-year-old seminary graduates to think in terms of retirement, but that is when the groundwork is laid. Planning begins with the first deferred payment into the denominational pension plan or a 403(B) or a mortgage.

Planning for "meaningful" retirement is a challenge. What is "meaningful" retirement? It involves (1) a purpose and mission, and (2) economic security. A lack of purpose can result in illness or even early death. Such a lack can easily develop unless retirement is viewed as an important stage of personal development. A lack of financial security can undermine all the purpose in planning.

The failure to integrate these two factors accounts for the fact that a satisfying retirement seems to elude many clergy. We don't reach that goal by starting our planning at sixty years of age. It begins in early adulthood, when the career is just getting under way.

Every pastor should plan a retirement program with the participation and cooperation of whatever church he is ministering to at any given time.

GUIDELINES FOR PLANNING RETIREMENT

Let's look at some principles for retirement planning.

1. *Do not expect social security to be the only source of retirement income.* This may no longer be the expectation among younger clergy, but there are thousands of fifty- and sixty-year-old ministers who early in their careers thought social security would be an adequate base for retirement income.

Even though the U.S. Congress has keyed increases in social security benefits to the Consumer Price Index (CPI), the amounts still will not allow for a comfortable retirement. A clergyman and his spouse retiring today can count on about $10,000 to $12,000 per year from social security. Few retirees can live comfortably on that amount. Therefore, social security must be viewed as a component and not the sole source.

Consider the example of a pastor who, just twenty-five years ago at age forty, invested $2,000 per year in a mutual fund that returned an average of about 12 percent annually in interest and capital gains. (There are numerous funds that have had this margin of return over that period of time). Now ready to retire, the pastor finds that the dollar amount has passed $300,000. This money invested, after taxes, at 8 percent would have produced nearly double the amount ($12,000) provided in social security payments. If the interest from this is used for living expenses, the couple still has a sizable estate to leave for their children and for God's work.

Let's look at another case. At age thirty a minister begins to invest $2,000 a year in a pension plan, 403(B), or IRA that returns 10 percent compounded annually. At age sixty-five he has a retirement fund in excess of $500,000. This amount, after taxes, could easily produce $32,000 per year in income, with the possibility of accumulating three times this amount.

Even though social security is not an adequate base for retirement, it is still wise for clergy to participate in that system, for reasons stated in the previous chapter.

2. *Expect spending habits to change in retirement.* Most retired clergy will testify that spending habits change during retirement. It may not be *less* spending, but *different*.

First, if we have planned successfully, we will spend nothing or very little on life insurance. There obviously is no need to be purchasing life insurance if we have a retirement fund that will outlive us and our mate. We will probably spend less on food, since older families tend to eat less. Even "eating out" can cost less with senior citizen discounts and "early bird" meals.

Expenses are likely to be higher as regards leisure and recreation. This is due to having more time, freedom, and perhaps money to travel. Visits to children, grandchildren, or friends may prove to be economical.

Housing is a major retirement decision. Clergy who have not owned a home must now provide housing. It is usually wiser to rent in retirement than to buy. A clergyman who is already a home owner may decide to sell and then purchase a home or condominium in a warmer climate.

Business and clergy expenses will be negligible. And you will no longer be paying into a retirement program.

The fact is that spending habits will begin to change with the first day of retirement.

3. *Involve your spouse in all retirement planning.* Retirement plans should be thoroughly discussed with your mate. Beginning discussion well before retirement will eliminate potential arguments. Often you will find your spouse both highly knowledgeable and highly interested, because this crucial change in lifestyle affects one spouse as much as the other. Every spouse should know full details of all financial plans throughout life, and that of course includes retirement.

A man should anticipate that his wife will outlive him. In 1984 the actuary tables revealed that women outlived men on the average of about 6½ years. Condominiums and retirement villages in the "Sun Belt" inevitably have a higher proportion of widows than widowers.

This reality must guide our planning. We must plan so that our retirement funds will not be depleted or greatly diminished at death. It is important to be informed on a denominational pension plan. Most plans allow a one-time distribution, a ten-year payment, or the option of one or two payments. This will be explained later in detail.

Including your spouse in retirement planning will make that stage of life more enjoyable and satisfying for both.

4. *Estimate your projected income and expenses five to ten years before retirement.* Estimating how you will live in retirement is not as difficult as it may seem. Adjustments to retirement plans can be made a few years before, but only if you carefully estimate your income and expenses. A look ahead is important.

In making these calculations, include the following:

Estimated pension/annuity	$ _____
Estimated 403(B)/IRA	$ _____
Estimated interest/dividends	$ _____
Estimated social security	$ _____
Estimated part-time/other	$ _____
	$ _____
Total retirement income	$ _____

You may question whether to include a part-time salary, but consider that nearly every pastor is called upon to serve as a pulpit supply, an interim pastor, or a visitation pastor in the early retirement years. This is a mental and financial benefit that is somewhat unique to clergy; part-time employment keeps the ministerial skills active besides providing some additional income.

The expense side of the ledger may be more difficult to estimate. Usually retirees can maintain their lifestyle on 75 to 80 percent of their last annual, full-time salary. This simply means that expenses may be 20 to 25 percent lower in retirement, and we saw earlier in this chapter why that is a reasonable assumption, though it is not always the case.

Inflation must be considered in estimating the retirement budget. The rate of inflation fluctuates, but a good rule of thumb is to estimate 5 percent a year over ten years. This means the retirement account must provide 5 percent more income each year to maintain your lifestyle. The "Rule of 72" is helpful; this is a mathematical device that answers the question, "How long will it take for my money to double at various rates of return?" You can determine what retirement dollars will be needed by estimating the annual inflation rate and dividing it into 72. For example, a rate of 6 percent divided into 72 equals 12 years; a rate of 5.5 percent equals 14.4 years.

You and your spouse can expect to live fifteen or twenty years beyond retirement. The answer to the inflation problem is met only in a retirement fund that exceeds the needs of the first few years or that appreciates even after retirement begins. The latter is achievable, but it requires diligent attention.

5. *Carefully determine the best payout formula of the retirement funds.* An important decision to make just before retiring is the choice of terms for pension payout. Most denominational and educational funds (Teachers Insurance and Annuity) allow for a number of options at retirement. Several options are generally available.

OPTIONS FOR RETIREMENT FUNDING

Single Lump Sum Payout

In a single lump sum payout, all the accrued dollars, less any service charges, are returned to you at one time. There are some distinct disadvantages with this option. First, you may face a heavy tax liability, since this money represents deferred income. Second, you must decide what to do with this lump sum when you get it. You can offset the tax liability only by leaving in the retirement fund all but the first year's needed income. So the tax liability and other tax regulations may make a single lump payment undesirable.

Single Life Option

Most pension plans offer a variety of vesting plans. One is the single life option. Under this plan you will be paid a designated annual amount for as long as you live. Some plans offer options that are modifications of this, namely, a "guaranteed" or "non-guaranteed" plan. "Non-guaranteed" means that the benefits stop when you die, even though your spouse is still living. "Guaranteed" provides for benefits for a fixed period, such as ten years, regardless of how long you live. The annual distribution of income is higher in the non-guaranteed option, but the risk of loss is obviously higher. The guaranteed option assures your spouse or estate an income for a fixed number of years.

Joint Life Option

Another vesting plan is the joint life option, which provides benefits as long as either you or your spouse is living. Some plans reduce the benefit after the vested person dies. Check the terms of your plan before retirement. The "guaranteed" and "non-guaranteed" parts work the same as under the single life option.

I prefer the guaranteed joint life option. While the benefits may decline by about 12 percent per year, it assures us of income until death—which, remember, might well come as long as fifteen to twenty years after retirement.

Plans such as a 403(B) and an IRA work on different rules. First, a 403(B), set up by the church and you, will probably be invested in mutual funds. In retirement you may withdraw only the amount of money you will need for one year. The withdrawal may be made monthly, quarterly, or annually. You will pay tax on whatever you withdraw, but the rest of the account continues to grow. For example, suppose a minister has accumulated $150,000 in XYZ mutual fund by the time he retires. He estimates the cost of living in retirement will be $30,000 a year.

Social security	$12,000
Part-time work	4,500
Interest/dividends	1,500
403(B)/IRA funds	12,000
Total	$30,000

Given the fact that there are also dividends, the $150,000 investment would need to appreciate only 8 percent per year. The result is that the minister would still have $150,000 in the XYZ fund available for withdrawal and some appreciation every year, without loss of principal.

That explains why I myself have planned for a combination of fixed income annuity and the flexibility of a 403(B) fund that allows for appreciation and growth during retirement years. The 403(B) distribution must begin by age seventy, according to present tax guidelines.

IRA funds, after age 59½, work basically the same way, but must be fully paid out by age 70½.

Always plan in advance for retirement and its options. Keep current with your social security account, checking every three years that the payments have been properly accounted for. After three years you have no recourse for amending errors. Your local office will help you get the needed information, or write to:

Social Security Administration
Department of Public Inquiries
6401 Security Blvd.
Baltimore, MD 21235

DECIDING WHERE TO LIVE

There are a number of factors to consider in deciding where to settle down for retirement. It involves more than heading for the sun.

Many "northern" retirees will move south or southwest due to the attraction of the Sun Belt. A few clergy will have the option to live in the Sun Belt from November to May and spend summer and early fall in another climate. Yet most will be forced to confine themselves to one home, and therefore location becomes primary.

It is best to rate the priority of several factors in retirement planning. Both spouses must be in clear agreement on these:

Family location

Friends proximity
Opportunity for part-time work
Favorable climate
Medical resources
Cultural/educational resources

Other items may be added to the list. However many there are, rank them in order of importance. This helps to lead to some firm decisions. In our own case, proximity to family is a minor consideration, since two of our three children are pastors and will have some mobility; we had better plan a travel budget to allow visits.

Should pastors retire in the last community they have served? Probably not, out of fairness to the new pastor as well as because of the adjustments that come with leaving the active ministry. Why try to make these adjustments in the shadow of your last pastorate?

In two instances my predecessors in the pastorate returned to the church after retirement. The potential for discomfort was alleviated because they both spent three to five years away from the church before returning. This period bridged the situation for both themselves and me as the current pastor. Each man, at my suggestion, was named "Pastor Emeritus." Our relationship was excellent.

It is wise to spend vacation time in the proposed retirement area both in season and out of season. Know the area before making a final decision.

A growing option is investment in a retirement center. Scores of these have opened in the last twenty years, offering various options. Some require a large initial payment plus monthly charges without any recovery of the initial fee. Other recent plans include a higher initial fee plus monthly charge, but an estate recovery of up to 55 percent of the fee.

The following questions should be answered before making a commitment to a retirement center:

1. Does the facility have nursing and medical facilities available and included in the fee?

2. Is there sufficient recreation and planned activity to alleviate boredom?

3. Is the resident population compatible with my lifestyle? A denominational home may be preferred for this reason.

4. How does the contract handle potential increases in the monthly fee? Some centers confine rate increases to social security raises, which is to your advantage.

5. Does the facility offer a "meal plan" option? Many residents want to maintain their own kitchen, with the option of adopting a meal plan later on.

6. How often are the facilities refurbished, and who is responsible for this?

7. Who pays for the utilities?

8. Does the facility separate healthy retirees from residents who receive nursing care? A major complaint would be the antiseptic odor and depression of sickly people if the two groups are mixed.

9. Is transportation provided for shopping, entertainment, and church activities?

It is wise to make a decision regarding a retirement center before your children are forced to make it for you. The health and nursing care of a distant parent may impose an unnecessary burden on them.

Today some 30 million people in the United States are age sixty-five or over, and the number is growing. "Gray Power" is no longer idle talk: senior citizens have discount advantages, preferred federal housing, and societies such as the American Association of Retired People that lobby effectively for the retiree. It is interesting that senior citizens are increasingly designated as age fifty-five and older, yet many will live another thirty years—a third of a lifetime!

EXPENSES IN RETIREMENT

The Bureau of Labor Statistics has estimated the annual expenses of a typical retired couple in these percentages:

Housing	33%
Food	29%
Medical	10%
Transportation	10%
Clothing/personal care	7%
Family items (recreation, reading material, etc.)	5%
Other items (gifts, contributions, insurance)	6%

MAKING RETIREMENT JOYOUS

Retirement should never be a season of inactivity. Rather, it should be a time of freedom to change direction without economic burden. After all the decision-making on the matters already mentioned, there are still other ways to ensure a satisfying and rewarding retirement.

- Cultivate a hobby.
- Don't give up the opportunity to preach or teach when possible. God did not put an age limit on spiritual gifts.
- Adopt a younger clergy family and be their spiritual and moral support. How fulfilling and affirming for retirees!
- Retire where you have friends or family. Loneliness cannot be answered with dollars or climate.
- Plan for the day when you or your mate needs supportive care. A retirement center with nursing facilities is a splendid option. Look around well before the day of retirement.
- Don't be afraid to use your financial assets. You earned them. Your children would probably be more pleased to know you are comfortable than to receive a big inheritance from your estate.
- Travel while you are physically able. A friend of mine travels extensively at ninety years of age. Why not?
- Give to God's work liberally. Don't wait to give it all in bequest, when you can't enjoy the fruits of the gift. A friend of mine, now in his nineties, likes to say, "It is always better to give with the warm hand." This brother enjoys seeing the results of his gifts now.

- Be ready to live without a mate. This can best be developed by establishing a certain amount of "personal space" in retirement and not being overdependent on others.
- Be aware that you will soon be called to give account to God. The good steward receives the adulation, "Well done, good and faithful servant."

With good planning and forethought, retirement can be a fulfilling and crowning stage of a full and fruitful life of ministry.

14 | *THE WILL: A MOST IMPORTANT STATEMENT*

A will is not an optional matter, especially for anyone preaching and seeking to practice Christian stewardship. An estate is "intestate" if a person dies without a will; this means that heirs could be deprived of up to 50 percent of the assets by taxes and fees. That is hardly good stewardship.

But why is a will necessary? There are a number of reasons:

- Every estate is settled in a court of law;
- A will provides for the disposal or transfer of personal items such as remembrances;
- Percentage amounts left to children and other relatives are established;
- Percentage or dollar amounts left to a church, alma mater, or charities are established;
- Guardianship of minor children is determined;
- Funeral arrangements may be made.

Wills are customarily drafted with the aid of a lawyer, at a cost ranging from $40 to $300. Sometimes a denominational stewardship officer will care for this at little or no charge. In recent years, however, it has become legal literally to write one's own will by mail order at a cost of under $20; check whether your state has adopted legislation providing for this.

Each state has its own regulations regarding estates and wills. Clergy are in a special situation since they may move more often than the general population. Therefore, it is mandatory to update or evaluate your will in regard to the state law of your current residence.

Keeping a will up to date is important also because personal possessions change, responsibility for minor children changes as they reach adulthood, and personal wishes may also change as to the disposition of the estate.

A WILL AND PERSONAL RECORD KEEPING

Good records are always important, not least in regard to a will. It is a good idea to put an addendum to the will that lists personal property, life insurance policies by amount and number, retirement savings accounts, security holdings, and the deed for your gravesite. This addendum should be given to the executor, or at least he or she should be informed as to where both the will and the addendum are located.

A new concept that has become legal in most states is to make a video or audio tape that provides details on the location of records and personal items and the terms of disposal of the estate. This is useful and important in case of sudden or accidental death.

A witness or witnesses will be needed for the will, and it must be notarized. Witnesses should generally not be people who have an interest in the estate or are "in" the will.

CHOOSING AN EXECUTOR

An "executor" is legally charged to execute your wishes as described in the will. There are two lines of thought concerning the choice of an executor: (1) choose a noninvolved third party, such as a bank officer or a lawyer, or (2) choose a trusted relative or family friend, preferably younger than yourself.

The executor may receive fees as agreed upon by the court and within dollar limits set by law. Friends or relatives often waive this fee.

TAXES AND YOUR ESTATE

A will eliminates most tax liability, especially if the estate is valued at less than $800,000. State regulations vary on estate taxes, but a valid will alleviates the great risk of tax invasion of even a small estate.

GENERAL GUIDELINES

Since more than 90 percent of clergy are men, the following guidelines are directed chiefly to husbands:

1. Make a will at an early age and update it frequently.

2. Leave a detailed list of all insurance policies, their amounts, and where they are kept.

3. List all investments annually.

4. Update annually a recommended plan of estate investments for a two-year period. This will make a major decision easier for a widow, especially during a time of great stress.

5. Name a trusted friend, with financial acumen, in whom your widow may have confidence in seeking advice. Do not forget to advise your friend of your decision.

6. If possible, bequeath something to your denominational seminary, library fund, or another agency. The gift should be given in your memory. Often memorial gifts are requested at funerals instead of flowers.

Having worked hard to accumulate an estate, you exercise both good stewardship and common sense in providing a complete and up-to-date will. It is your last communication with your family. If you neglect a will, it may be your most costly act.

15 | ADVICE FOR LAY LEADERS

Clergy are "called of God" and there is no doubting their altruism, consecration, and dedication. Clergy commitment and dedication excels that of most other professions.

It is also true that clergy live in a "fishbowl." This lack of privacy is magnified when salaries are voted on by the congregation in many churches or are at least a matter of public record.

GUIDELINES FOR LAY STEWARDSHIP

How can lay leaders best exercise stewardship and responsibility in regard to the tithes and offerings of God's people and their biblical duty to care for God's servants? The following recommendations may be helpful to lay leaders and serve as a catalyst for discussion. Some of these topics are dealt with in earlier chapters, but are summarized here.

1. *A change of pastors should not mean a decline in salary for the new pastor.* The salary offered to a pastor should depend on the position that is being filled, his education and experience, and the economic conditions of the locale.

It is not uncommon for the departing pastor to discover that his successor will command a higher salary than he himself received. This may happen because the clergy financial package has not been adequately reviewed and updated. It is at the time of a change of position that ministers suddenly become aware of the reality of comparative salaries. Some churches have lost good pastors because they have not kept financial packages up to date.

2. *Church growth warrants financial reward for the pastor.* It is inconceivable that lay leaders would decline to share the increase of church and financial growth with the clergy staff—but some do!

All clergy should reap a normal increase based on the Consumer Price Index, but "merit" raises should also be provided, based on the congregation's numerical and spiritual growth and its satisfaction with pastoral performance.

3. *Seek to cover all business expenses of the pastor, preferably apart from salary.* A number of business expenses are sometimes "lumped" into a salary package. In the past, this had more tax advantages than at present. An annual report may give an unrealistic salary figure if all business expense items are included in the compensation. The Tax Reform Act of 1986 makes it important to have all business expenses reimbursed.

What should be considered a business expense assumed by the church? Even if a church cannot underwrite all the items listed below, they should be long-range goals.

- *Automobile expense.* There should be a monthly allowance that covers gas and oil, but also covers depreciation or a fixed amount per mile. The IRS allows 21 cents per mile up to 15,000 business miles and 11 cents for each additional mile. Car rental companies estimate the cost of maintenance and operation, including replacement, at between 30 and 45 cents per mile. Some churches have leased a car for their pastor.
- *Conference and denominational expense.* A church should want its pastor to represent it at denominational meetings. The expense should be included in the church budget; consider paying the spouse's expenses also. This action pays dividends to the church, the clergy, and the denomination. The pastor's time spent in these activities should not be counted as vacation.

- *Continuing education.* A plan should be set up with an appropriate budget for continuing education mutually agreed on by the church and the pastor. The time should not be designated as vacation. The plan should designate how much, if any, of the cost will be borne by the church. Clergy must keep intellectually fit and educationally up to date. It is really a necessity now, not an option. The educational and practical expertise gained will profit the church.
- *Book allowance.* Books are clergy's tools of the trade. A church that is able to provide a book allowance will receive the benefit. The amount may begin at a modest level and then be gradually increased. Set guidelines for book purchases and for ownership of the books when the church-pastor relationship ends.
- *Insurance/retirement.* Hospitalization insurance is mandatory. Earlier in this book I suggested that clergy consider other coverage, certain kinds of which should be paid by the church. Among preferred coverages: (1) term life insurance (as much as $100,000), (2) disability insurance (which benefits both church and pastor), (3) retirement plan (with a minimum goal of 10 percent of salary), and (4) professional liability insurance (protection for counseling and pastoral advice).
- *Entertainment allowance.* Few laypeople understand how much and how often clergy "entertain" at their own expense. Visiting clergy, missionaries, or speakers are often assumed to be the responsibility of the pastor. The wise and thoughtful church will reimburse the pastor monthly for this expense. Include in this "business meals," such as meetings with church members or constituency that involves church business.
- *Other expenses.* There are other matters that thoughtful lay leaders should consider, such as computers, sabbatical options, and travel allowance.

4. *Formally evaluate and review the clergy and ministry staff annually.* All people who are employed by others need review. This review will sensitively examine the strengths

and weaknesses of your pastor. If this is done annually and prior to, but in connection with, the salary review, then the experience does not need to become confrontative. Often the suggestion to evaluate the pastor arises only when someone is dissatisfied with his ministry. Annual reviews alleviate that risk. This does not mean an annual "vote of confidence" by the congregation; the evaluation is best conducted by the proper church board with whatever input from the congregation is deemed helpful.

5. *Appoint a clergy relations committee.* The purpose of a relations committee is to seek to help the clergy family adjust to the changes inherent in accepting a new call; to provide oversight of parsonage needs; to aid in entertainment; to assist communication and avert misunderstandings; and to contribute to the annual evaluation. To whom do clergy go with a "house problem" or a financial concern? A clergy relations committee can prevent many problems and alleviate much criticism.

6. *Keep the clergy financial information confidential.* Should every member know the pastor's salary and benefit package? Every member has the right to know, but it is my conviction that the amount should not be published or isolated from other statistics. If there is more than one staff person, all the salaries should be included on one line in the budget, "pastoral and staff salaries." The percentage of salary raises will be of interest even where the specific dollar amounts are not published. If a member desires to know specific dollar amounts, he or she should make the request in writing to the proper board or officer.

I have visited churches where annual reports are available to all visitors, and the report gives full information on pastoral salaries. This is information best kept private to leadership and available on request to the congregation, but certainly not shared outside the membership.

Smaller churches probably compensate the pastor at median levels of the community. Larger churches with multiple staff will have clergy compensated above the mean. This is difficult for many members to accept. But the church is in many ways like a small business. Also, clergy are a part of our economic system that responds to the laws of supply and demand.

A senior pastor should be compensated higher than other professional staff. Similar benefits should be available to all, but the levels of compensation or participation may vary due to responsibility, training, and experience. Usually the difference between senior pastor and other staff will range from 15 to 30 percent; I believe 15 percent should be the minimum differential.

7. *Clearly define the terms of employment.* Chapter 3 should be read by church leaders. Most employment problems arise from a failure to communicate clearly on financial matters, job expectations, and goals. Misunderstandings can abound when communication is nebulous. Every pastor and church should have a signed "letter of agreement" that defines the terms of employment at the time a pastoral relationship is entered into. Such a letter will avert most misunderstandings.

8. *Allow the pastor to be informed and knowledgeable about church finances.* Many church leaders believe that clergy should leave the financial matters of the church to lay leaders. Some officers are offended that a pastor should be involved in church finances. But are not the financial and spiritual matters of the church tied together? It is interesting that often, when church giving declines, the pastor has to shoulder much of the blame.

Clergy should be not only informed but knowledgable about financial matters. They should know how to read a balance sheet and a profit/loss statement. The church should expect this of them. Pastors must remember that one of their roles is similar to the chief executive officer of a small business.

Budget formation must always include the senior pastor's counsel and opinion.

9. *Give the clergy family freedom to live a Christian lifestyle.* Clergy families are often subjected to the scrutiny of many

eyes in regard to their spending and lifestyle. The primary concern of the church should be simply, does the clergy family exhibit a Christian lifestyle? It is not the right or privilege of church members to critique the purchases or spending habits of the pastor and family, unless they differ from Christian lifestyle.

The clergy family have a right to prioritize their spending without second-guessing from the congregation. Frequently such matters as the choice of automobile, the quality of clothing, or the kind of vacation will come under scrutiny. (" 'Poor pastors' shouldn't go to Florida or Hawaii!") Do not allow this criticism to become gossip.

The congregation should be reminded that the pastor has stewardship responsibilities for the paycheck, and that means accountability primarily to God and secondarily to the church.

The expectations of what a Christian lifestyle consists of should be reasonable and biblical. Some suggestions are that the pastor should—

- Practice thrift, not extravagance—but often this is in the eye of the beholder.
- Pay his bills punctually. The testimony of church and clergy is sometimes ruined in a community because of unpaid clergy bills.
- Care materially for his family. They should not have to be the recipients of every piece of secondhand clothing in the congregation.
- Set an example in tithe and offerings. A pastor's model in giving is important.
- Plan wisely for retirement so that a burden of care will not rest on the church. This is only possible if the church provides its fair share of investment.

I am concerned that many P.K.s (pastors' kids) have been soured on ministry and the church because of criticism from the congregation. This criticism often involves spending, but it should not and does not need to be true. Would lay leaders like their spending habits and handling of money put under scrutiny?

10. *Do not make the pastor the major contributor to missions and the building fund.* There are pastors who have not received an annual salary increase but have listened as missionary support was increased or added. How unfair! How can a church justify an increase in missionary support and have less regard for the pastor, who, after all, is the person most directly accountable to the congregation? I am not suggesting that churches be less considerate of missions; rather, this is a reminder that mission boards are sometimes more caring and responsive to the financial needs of missionaries than churches are to their pastors'. Both missionaries and pastors should be paid and raised justifiably and proportionately.

A building program is also a potential source of trouble in clergy finances. A congregation once told me that because of the pending building project and accompanying mortgage, a proposed 10 percent raise was cut to 5 percent. The raise would have been about $2,000 but was reduced to $1,000; therefore, in effect, I was contributing $1,000 to the building program without my consent. When I challenged every leader of the church to promise to give 50 percent of their next raise to the building fund, they restored my raise to 10 percent. They realized that they wanted me to do what they would not do themselves.

Asking the pastor to make the major sacrifice often happens at the time of a call. One church called me, but offered $100 per month less than the church I was pastoring at the time. Their justification was that they had a heavy mortgage, and they asked me to commit to a spirit of sacrifice. I had been told that 104 households gave regularly to the church. I challenged the call committee to make an equal sacrifice: why should the appeal involve only the pastor? If each contributor added one more dollar per month to their giving, I would sacrifice $1 per month from my salary. The call letter came back with my promised salary $100 a month higher!

The point is that church leaders sometimes fail to consider all the implications of their decisions. I hope this counsel will make them more sensitive to the matter of clergy finances.

11. *Pray for the pastor and encourage him in special ways.*
Prayer is the backbone of spiritual life. A regular prayer time
for pastor and staff will do much to care for problems. My
father, who served as a church leader for much of his life,
often said, "Touch not the Lord's anointed," whenever
criticism was directed toward the pastor. And no one prayed
for the pastor more specifically and more often than my
father. Prayer accomplishes its purpose.

Encouragement takes many forms, but should always
be sincere. A note of thanks for a sermon or another act of
ministry has lifted me in a depressed time. For years we have
received annually a Thanksgiving floral plant from a parishioner of a time past. Why not honor the pastor's birthday
with a card shower or treat his family to a night out?

Probably no one encounters the emotional highs and
lows in vocation as much as clergy. Prayers and acts of
encouragement help greatly. I know this from experience.

THE HOUSING QUESTION

We could add one more guideline to the foregoing:
*Evaluate the housing question periodically, whether the church or
the clergy owns the house the clergy lives in.* Because there are
many factors to consider in clergy housing, it seems wise to
deal with the matter separately.

A church must decide whether or not it should provide
a parsonage. In rural areas and small towns where resale may
be slow, it is to the benefit of the church and clergy to have
church ownership. Where equity advances and homes sell
more quickly, as in urban and suburban areas, pastor
ownership may be more advantageous to all. If the pastor
owns a home, the church should make allowances, as
suggested in chapter 8.

Whatever the case, it is important to guard the privacy
of the home. The church may own the home, but it is the
"castle" of the pastor; the family should have a sense of
living in freedom. Respect the fact that "drop-in" visits from
church leaders or other laypeople can be inconvenient,
disruptive, and sometimes just plain irritating.

Church Ownership

In church ownership, the congregation should consider extra compensation for the pastor as its equity in the home rises. The pastor will not benefit from that equity except through an "equity adjustment" to the salary of perhaps 3 to 5 percent a year. This might well be assigned to the clergy retirement account or set aside in a special fund toward a future down payment on a home of his own.

Some other factors should be considered in regard to church ownership. In particular, lay leaders should—

- *Allow latitude in decorating and refurbishing.* Let the "family personality" be expressed, within limits. A change of pastors should be accompanied with a change of decor if the new clergy family desires it, and the family should play a role in making decisions about it. The church should plan to redecorate for the same family after perhaps five to seven years.
- *Keep the home in good repair.* There should be an annual maintenance inspection. The home is a reflection of the church. If utilities are paid by the pastor, make sure that all necessary precautions are taken to ensure that insulation, storm windows, and the like are helping to reduce utility costs.
- *Define clearly all responsibilities so that misunderstandings are kept to a minimum.* A parsonage committee is an important consideration.
- *Consider paying or sharing utility costs.* Additionally, note that the church receives direct benefit from the telephone.

Clergy Ownership

If the pastor and the church are agreed on clergy ownership of housing, there are several things to consider to ensure fair financial responsibility.

1. *It may be appropriate to lend the pastor a down payment for housing.* This could be important as the clergy decides whether to accept a call. It might well lessen anxiety on the part of the pastor and family in the transition. Most churches

can make such a loan available at little or no interest. The most progressive churches set a timetable for gradually forgiving part of this loan based on length of service.

2. *Another way of fulfilling this down payment loan is through an agreed equity appreciation share upon sale and without an interest on the loan.* For example, the church offers a $15,000 loan at no interest; but ten years later, when the pastor moves and sells the home, it has appreciated from $75,000 to $100,000. The church provided $15,000, or 20 percent of the original home cost; the equity gain was $25,000 after all selling expenses. Therefore, the church receives back the original $15,000 plus 20 percent of $25,000 (that is, $5,000). The pastor leaves with $20,000 for a new home plus equity. The church has an immediate $20,000 to lend to the next pastor. This is a simple, fair, and realistic plan for many churches.

3. *Suggest and make available the church's bank relationship for a home loan.* Many banks will give favorable rates and allow a smaller down payment if the church does its banking with the institution. If there is a question of credit, why not have the church guarantee the loan?

4. *Arrange a home buy-back contract with the pastor when he begins his ministry.* This is an ordinary contract that pledges the church to purchase the home from the pastor at the time the pastoral relationship ends, with the price to be based on the average amount of three appraisals.

With this commitment from the church, a pastor is less likely to feel bound to remain in his position longer than he should. The church can rent or sell the property at leisure or keep it for the next pastor as an option. This protection will serve both the church and the pastor well.

CONCLUSION

I hope this chapter will be put into the hands of many church leaders. It should be reviewed by every officer, especially those assuming duties for the first time. While there may be room for disagreement on some specifics, I promise that if these general guidelines are followed, the result will be a more confident pastor and family. The result may be even more effective service.

16 | QUESTIONS AND ANSWERS ON FINANCES

1. Should I join an HMO?

HMO (Health Maintenance Organization) plans are a fairly recent development and are popular across the United States. Some areas offer numerous choices in HMOs.

An HMO differs from a conventional health insurance plan in that it emphasizes health maintenance and illness prevention. HMOs take various forms, and they may or may not save money compared with a standard health policy. The HMO reduces costs only if the present medical policy does not include "prevention visits." Under the HMO the doctor's office is available without additional charge; under most regular health policies there are either restrictions or deductibles in force.

Is an HMO the right plan for you? If you want to choose your own doctor, you may not desire an HMO. However, it is always possible that the medical staff on the HMO list includes your doctor.

Most HMOs do not have deductibles or co-payments. Usually an HMO premium is about the same or slightly higher than regular health insurance. The advantage lies in health maintenance and the prevention of illness.

There are two types of HMO plans: (1) doctors in an HMO group see patients in a central facility; the group has its own specialists and a limited choice of hospitals; (2) an IPA (Independent Practice Association) contracts with a number of doctors in all specialties and in general practice; a number of hospital choices are under contract.

Quality varies widely among HMO plans. There are a number of questions to ask in deciding whether to join an HMO:

- Is there a good diversity of specialties available?
- How does the plan handle second opinions?
- Which hospitals does the HMO use?
- How far must I travel to the doctors and the hospital?
- How long must I wait for an appointment?

There may be little advantage in an HMO for clergy who receive free or liberally discounted medical care. Probably the best advantage is health maintenance.

2. Should a child receive an allowance, and if so, how much?

About 90 percent of parents give some form of an allowance to children, according to a survey conducted by *Working Mother* magazine. Allowances are usually initiated at ages six to eight.

Children should receive allowances for no other reason than to teach them money management at an early age. The amount of the allowance is secondary to the fact that the child must do some budgeting.

The same survey disclosed that 74 percent of the children spend some or all of their money on toys. Some 43 percent bought food. About 19 percent bought school supplies, and 39 percent bought gifts for others. Only 15 percent had any savings from the allowance.

The allowances averaged from $1.40 per week for six-year-olds to above $8.00 per week for teens ages sixteen and older. In a clergy family, amount will be determined by income and what a child is expected to provide out of the allowance. If items such as school lunches and bus fares are to be paid from the allowance, then the amount must be high enough to allow the child ample "discretionary" funds.

Two principles must be taught through an allowance. First, God's share must be allocated by the child. The dime out of every dollar that is personally put into the offering plate each Sunday is a valuable teaching aid.

The second principle relates to systematic savings. Children should learn at an early age the significance of saving a proportion (preferably at least 10 percent) of income. Spending habits and traits will carry over into adulthood, so it is important that children get started right. An allowance begins the process. If children run out of money, let them learn the discipline of careful spending, either by leaving their "shortfall" unfunded or by insisting that they borrow at interest. This is not merely "kiddie economics"; children learn fast and can set patterns for life.

3. May I hire my spouse or my child to work for me?

As a self-employed person you may hire your spouse or a child, but there are rules that apply: (1) they may be paid no more than comparative wages for such work; (2) you must contribute social security payments as an employer; this is easily accomplished through the social security office; (3) a record of hours worked must be kept; and (4) in some states, workmen's compensation must be paid.

What are the advantages? There are several: (1) the spouse may begin an IRA as long as the earnings are over $2,000 per year and other criteria are met; (2) the spouse's earnings may be written off as a business expense, thereby reducing the family's adjusted gross income; and (3) the spouse accrues more quarters toward a higher benefit from social security.

Jobs that fit well for this kind of employment are typing, computer entry, or filing. These would fall within the lines of self-employed expense for clergy and institutional faculty.

4. Must I report as income my gifts from funerals and weddings?

This is a difficult decision to make. It really is determined by whether the gift is a "fee" for "services rendered." If a funeral home reimburses you, it is clearly a fee; if a family offers a card and money, it is probably a gift.

I report all these funds as income, but even so there are allowable deductions, such as pay for a baby-sitter during a rehearsal dinner and wedding. Another solution to the situation is to turn all these funds over to the church to be placed in a restricted account for clergy expense such as books. This allows you to use the money, but it is not considered income.

As a general rule, an error in favor of the IRS allows you to sleep better at night.

5. Is buying an extended warranty for a new car profitable?

All dealers offer an extended warranty policy for the purchase of a new automobile. A contract may cost from $200 to $1,100 depending on its term, which may range from two to five (more recently, up to seven) years.

It is important to understand clearly what is and is not covered under the warranty. Such items as brakes, exhaust systems, and shock absorbers are often excluded; and in fact, many warranties cover virtually the major drive train only. A warranty begins on the date that the vehicle is first driven, so a four-year policy purchased six months later really has only 3½ years of life.

These warranty policies generally work to the advantage of the manufacturer/dealer and insurance companies. Certain manufacturers now offer up to a 70,000-mile or seven-year warranty included in the price of the car. That is the best deal in terms of protection.

6. How much will term insurance cost me?

Obviously, insurance rates vary widely according to specific terms of a policy and the carrier. The following table applies to a guaranteed renewable policy, nonsmoker, lowest premium first year:

Age	$100,000	$250,000	$500,000
25	$92	$185	$300
30	94	185	300
35	95	185	300

40	140	240	430
45	152	320	695
50	203	475	1,000
55	296	680	1,540
60	469	1,087	2,355
65	822	1,905	3,655

A comparison of the figures shows that the $100,000 policy costs $9.20 per thousand dollars of coverage, the $250,000 coverage costs just over $8.00 per thousand, and the $500,000 policy drops to $6.00. The last is the best buy, of course. If the budget can handle the premium, it is the right option. Always figure out the cost per thousand on term insurance and shop for the best deal.

7. If my bank fails, is my money safe?

Up to $100,000 is insured if the institution is a member of the Federal Deposit Insurance Corporation (FDIC) or Federal Savings and Loan Insurance Corporation (FSLIC).

The only inconvenience that might result from a bank failure is a slight delay in getting access to your money. Nearly 150 banks failed in 1986 compared with 10 closings in 1980, but this may be due to a readjustment phase in the economy. The burden of loss falls most on the institutions' shareholders, since they are last in line and are uninsured.

8. What is a living trust?

A living trust is a trust set up as a means to reduce the cost of probate and preserve more of the estate for your heirs. You may name yourself as the beneficiary and name a trustee to manage your assets in case of disability or death.

Trusts can be set up as "irrevocable" (unchangeable) or "revocable" (subject to change by you). A living trust is the revocable type and offers the following advantages:

- Flexibility to make changes
- Avoiding most probate costs
- Privacy of estate at death, since it does not become a probate record

- Assets under control of the family or charity, avoiding court or transfer fees
- Avoiding most tax liability

I suggest having both a will and a living trust, since some nonfinancial matters such as guardianship of minor children are the province of the former only.

9. What is a "home equity loan"?

An equity loan is essentially a second mortgage on a property. For example, you may have a $50,000 mortgage on a home currently appraised at $100,000. A lending institution will offer a second mortgage for the difference between $50,000 and 80 percent ($80,000) of the home's appraised value. This means you could borrow $30,000 without disturbing your primary or first mortgage.

This action immediately lowers the equity in the home. If you need to borrow a large sum for something like education or medical bills, this type of loan is generally less expensive than a conventional one. The interest is also tax deductible under IRS rules if the loan is used for medical or educational purposes. The loan cannot be higher than the cost of purchase and improvements made over the years of your ownership. Such loans will generally carry an interest rate somewhat higher than that on the first mortgage.

10. What are "points" in relation to a home mortgage?

"Points" are simply a percentage of the mortgage added to the closing costs over and above the mortgage principal and interest. It is virtually a handling fee for the mortgage lender, and it is usually paid at the time of closing. One point is equal to one percent of the amount of money borrowed.

When mortgage money is readily available, the points on loans will decrease; conversely, a tight market means there will be more points.

Suppose you are taking out a $50,000 mortgage at 9½ percent interest, one point, for thirty years. A "point fee" of $500 (1 percent of $50,000) will be assessed, or the lender may give you the option of a mortgage of $50,000 at 10 percent, no points, for thirty years. Which is the better deal? They are about equal in this case, so can choose to pay the 1 percent up front in closing, or amortize it.

Always inquire about the rate of the mortgage, the life of the mortgage, and the number of points.

11. Is it profitable to assume an existing mortgage?

Assuming a mortgage, which means transferring the loan from the seller to you, the buyer, is usually profitable, because inflation is likely to make the interest rate on a new loan higher than the rate on an old loan. But there are some qualifications. Inflation also tends to increase the equity in the home. Therefore a higher down payment may be required, because you as the buyer have to satisfy the difference between your purchase price and the seller's value. For example, a new mortgage would require only a $20,000 down payment on a home worth $100,000; but because of the seller's equity and low remaining principal, you need to provide $35,000 in cash to assume the mortgage.

Now, is it better to acquire an $80,000 mortgage at 10 percent than to assume the owner's mortgage at $65,000 at 8 percent interest? Yes, if you cannot earn more than 8 percent growth on the extra $15,000. Remember also that the larger mortgage payment means you are paying more interest that is tax deductible and can be designated as housing allowance. Thus it is hard to tell which route is more beneficial.

Of course, the decision-making process depends on your having the extra cash available. In recent years, moreover, many mortgage institutions have made it more difficult to assume mortgages under the old rates.

12. Is it better to buy a new home or a used home?

Many positive and negative factors must be weighed in choosing between these alternatives.

NEW HOME

Plus: No major repairs or replacement for first few years
Choice of decor and extras
Some choice of design and plan

Minus: Additional costs for landscaping, drapes, and other
          items that may not have been considered
          Location perhaps isolated from shopping and bereft of
          trees and vegetation
          No opportunity to assume a mortgage
          Perhaps need to choose between a second car and
          higher transportation costs

USED HOME

Plus: Mature landscaping
          Mature neighborhood with services available
          Cost negotiable
          Many fixtures included: drapery rods, drapes,
          extra towel bars and cabinets, hooks, garage or
          shed additions

Minus: Choice between existing decor and paying for
          redecorating
          Possible repairs and replacement of roof, bath-
          rooms, heating unit

It has been our experience that new homes are fun to plan and occupy, but used homes entail less anxiety, especially in moving to a new community.

13. What are "penny stocks"?

It seems that clergy often get hooked on the "penny stock market." These are usually low-priced (under two dollars) venture capital companies—new firms that sell stock to raise start-up money. For years the penny stock market has centered in Denver; these stocks are often unlisted in the major markets.

The dream is that the stock that stands at 10 cents a share now will someday reach $10. The problem is that most stocks of this nature fall or discontinue; only a small number rise very quickly.

Clergy should avoid get-rich-quick ideas and gambling. I view the penny stock market as dangerously close to both.

APPENDIX A: CALCULATING YOUR NET WORTH

This worksheet will help you to figure your net worth and compare yourself with other Americans. Calculate your assets, then subtract the sum of your liabilities.

ASSETS

Personal property:

Market value of home   _____

Market value of car 1   _____

Market value of car 2   _____

Market value of other tangible personal prop- _____
 erty

   TOTAL PERSONAL PROPERTY   _____

Cash:

Bank accounts and certificates   _____

Money market funds   _____

   TOTAL CASH   _____

Investments:

Stocks and mutual funds   _____

Real estate (other than home)   _____

Cash value of life insurance   _____

Other income   _____

   TOTAL INVESTMENTS   _____

Retirement assets:

IRAs   _____

Employee retirement plans/403(B)   _____

   TOTAL RETIREMENT ASSETS   _____

Total Assets   _____

LIABILITIES

Home mortgage   _____

Other mortgages   _____

Car loans   _____

Other consumer loans   _____

Educational loans   _____

Other: _____

Total Liabilities   _____

Net Worth   _____

COMPARING NET WORTH

Age of head of household	Median net worth
Under 35	$6,739
35 to 44	41,959
45 to 54	55,509
55 to 64	68,608
65 or older	53,982

(Source: *Ft. Lauderdale News/Sun/Sentinel* [5 January 1987])

APPENDIX B: HOW TO READ THE FINANCIAL PAGES

If you thought Greek and Hebrew were confusing on first encounter in seminary, try reading the financial pages of the newspaper! Clergy are not taught to understand the financial world in their professional training, but it is important to do so to keep track of investments.

A number of symbols are commonly used in the stock pages of newspapers. Three major exchanges are listed daily in most city newspapers, with full listings in the *Wall Street Journal*.

THE MAJOR STOCK EXCHANGES

New York Stock Exchange (NYSE)

The listing of the New York Stock Exchange in the financial pages will be for the composite tables of trades made the preceding day on the New York, Philadelphia, Boston, Midwest, Cincinnati, and Pacific stock exchanges. The NYSE is the largest exchange and represents the major corporations in the United States.

American Stock Exchange (AMEX)

The number of stocks listed on the American Stock Exchange may be significantly smaller than those on the NYSE, and the companies may also be smaller. The AMEX features many oil, metal, and electronic companies. The listings come from the same sources as the NYSE.

NASDAQ

The youngest exchange has a fine growth record. The National Association of Securities Dealers Automated Quotation System, commonly known as NASDAQ, is basically the over-the-counter, or secondary, market. For some time after its founding it was thought of as less than attractive, but it has gained major importance. It usually lists companies of smaller size and new venture capital companies. These are usually the high-growth, higher-risk companies that are the products of venture capital.

COMMON SYMBOLS IN STOCK REPORTS

The following symbols are generally used in newspapers for stock reports of each exchange. Note that a listing will be reporting on the preceding day's stock activity.

PE The company's price-to-earnings ratio, derived by figuring the price per share against earnings for the fiscal year.

HDS The number of shares sold, usually multiplied by 100.

High, Low, Close A stock's highest, lowest, and final price per share for the (preceding) day's trading.

Chg The change between the preceding day's final price and the final price of the day before that.

u A notation that the stock set a new high in price for the year.

d A notation that the stock set a new low in price for the year.

e Dividend declared or paid during the preceding twelve months.

s A notation that a stock was split or divided, or a stock dividend of 25 percent or more was paid.

Stock prices are quoted in fractions and can be converted to dollars. For example, 45¼ = $45.25; 27⅞ = $27.87. A *pf* after a stock designates a preferred stock. These stocks are preferred before other (common) stocks when dividends are paid; that is, earnings must be distributed to the preferred stock first.

HOW TO READ MUTUAL FUNDS

Each mutual fund is identified under its family of funds. *Sell* is the price the investor will pay for a share in the fund. *Buy* is the price one must pay to buy a share. *NL,* or no change in price between buy and sell, means the fund does not have a "load," or a charge, for shares purchased.

Unlike the three major stock exchanges, the mutual fund listing is in dollars and cents.

Options, futures, and bonds will also be listed in most newspapers, but few clergy will have occasion to invest in these markets.

Reading the stock market pages may be of interest, but wise clergy will probably invest in stocks or mutual funds that do not need daily care and examination.

APPENDIX C: RESOURCES FOR FINANCIAL PLANNING

ORGANIZATIONS

American Association of Retired Persons
1909 K Street NW
Washington, DC 20049

American Council of Life Insurance
1850 K Street NW
Washington, DC 20006

Associated Credit Bureaus
P.O. Box 218300
Houston, TX 77218

College Board Early Financial Aid Planning Service
P.O. Box 2843
Princeton, NJ 08541

Consumer Information Center
Pueblo, CO 81009
(A catalog of government publications, and many publications themselves, is free of charge.)

Consumers Union
256 Washington Street
Mount Vernon, NY 10553

Early Planning for College Costs
P.O. Box 467
Rockville, MD 20850

Growth Stock Outlook

P.O. Box 15381
Chevy Chase, MD 20815

Institute of Certified Financial Planners
3443 South Galena / Suite 190
Denver, CO 80231

Student Financial Assistance
P.O. Box 84
Washington, DC 20044

PERIODICALS

Barron's Weekly
200 Burnett Road
Chicopee, MA 01021

Business Week
1221 Avenue of the Americas
New York, NY 10020

Forbes
60 Fifth Avenue
New York, NY 10011

Money
Time-Life Building
Rockefeller Center
New York, NY 10020

No-Load Fund Investor
P.O. Box 283
Hastings-on-Hudson, NY 10706

The Wall Street Journal
22 Cortlandt Street,
New York, NY, 10007

BIBLIOGRAPHY

Blue, Ron. *Master Your Money*. Nashville: Thomas Nelson, 1986.

Bowman, George M. *How to Succeed With Your Money*. Chicago: Moody, n.d.

Burkett, Larry. *The Financial Planning Workbook*. Christian Financial Concepts Series. Chicago: Moody, 1982.

_____. *How to Manage Your Money*. Christian Financial Concepts Series. Chicago: Moody, 1982.

_____. *Your Finances in Changing Times*. Rev. ed. Christian Financial Concepts Series. Chicago: Moody, 1982.

Casey, Douglas. *Strategic Investing*. New York: Pocket Books, 1982.

Clouse, Robert G. *Wealth and Poverty*. Downers Grove, Ill.: InterVarsity, 1984.

Currier, Chet. *The Investor's Encyclopedia*. New York: Franklin Watts, 1985.

Dayton, Howard L., Jr. *Your Money: Frustration or Freedom? The Biblical Guide to Earning, Saving, Spending, Investing, Giving*. Wheaton, Ill.: Tyndale House, 1986.

Fooshee, George, Jr. *You Can Be Financially Free: Practical Christian Principles for Handling Your Family Finances*. Old Tappan, N.J.: Fleming H. Revell, 1976.

German, Don, and Joan German. *Money from A to Z: A Consumer's Guide to the Language of Personal Finance*. New York: Facts on File, 1984.

Griffiths, Brian. *The Creation of Wealth*. Downers Grove, Ill.: InterVarsity, 1984.

Hardy, C. Colburn. *Your Guide to a Financially Secure Retirement*. New York: Harper & Row, 1983.

Haughey, John C. *Holy Use of Money: Personal Finance in Light of Christian Faith*. Garden City, N.Y.: Doubleday, 1986.

Kilgore, James E. *Dollars and Sense: Making Your Money Work for You and Your Family.* Nashville: Abingdon, 1982.

Lasser, J. K. *What the New Tax Law Means to You.* New York: Pocket Books, 1986.

MacGregor, Malcolm. *Financial Planning Guide for Your Money Matters.* Minneapolis: Bethany House, 1981.

MacGregor, Malcolm, with Stanley C. Baldwin. *Your Money Matters.* Minneapolis: Bethany House, 1980.

McConaughy, David. *Money: The Acid Test.* New York: Missionary Education Movement of the United States and Canada, 1919.

Morgan, Darold H. *Personal Finances for Ministers.* Broadman Leadership Series. Nashville: Broadman, 1985.

Mumford, Amy Ross. *It Only Hurts Between Paydays.* Denver: Accent, 1986.

Nash, Ronald H. *Poverty and Wealth: The Christian Debate Over Capitalism.* Westchester, Ill.: Crossway, 1986.

Nauheim, Ferd. *The Retirement Money Book.* Washington: Acropolis, 1982.

North, Gary. *Honest Money: Biblical Principles of Money and Banking.* Biblical Blueprints Series. Nashville: Thomas Nelson, 1986.

————. *Successful Investing in an Age of Envy.* Nashville: Thomas Nelson, 1981.

Porter, Sylvia. *Sylvia Porter's New Money Book.* New York: Avon, 1986.

Prior, K. F. E. *God and Mammon: The Christian Mastery of Money.* Christian Foundations. Philadelphia: Westminster, 1965.

Rushford, Patricia H. *From Money Mess to Money Management.* Old Tappan, N.J.: Fleming H. Revell, Power Books, 1984.

Stillman, Richard J. *Guide to Personal Finance: A Lifetime Program of Money Management.* 4th ed. Englewood Cliffs, N.J.: Prentice-Hall, 1984.

Strassels, Paul N., and William B. Mead. *Money Matters. The Hassle-Free-Month-by-Month Guide to Money Management.* Washington: Addison-Wesley, 1986.

Van Caspel, Venita. *Money Dynamics for the New Economy.* New York: Simon & Schuster, 1986.

————. *The Power of Money Dynamics.* Englewood Cliffs, N.J.: Reston, 1983.

Vicker, Ray. *Dow-Jones Irwin Guide to Retirement Planning.* Homewood, Ill.: Dow-Jones, 1985.

Watkins, A. M. *How to Avoid the Biggest House-Buying Traps.* Rev. ed. Piermont, N.Y.: Building Institute, 1984.

Watts, John G. *Leave Your House in Order: A Guide to Planning Your Estate*. Rev. ed. Wheaton: Tyndale House, 1982.

Wilson, Ken. *Your Money and Your Life: Practical Guidance for Earning, Managing, and Giving Money*. Living as a Christian Series. Ann Arbor: Servant, 1983.